First World War
and Army of Occupation
War Diary
France, Belgium and Germany

3 CAVALRY DIVISION
Headquarters, Branches and Services
General Staff Appendices to 1141
4 May 1918 - 15 October 1918

WO95/1142/5

The Naval & Military Press Ltd
www.nmarchive.com
Published in association with The National Archives

Published by

The Naval & Military Press Ltd

Unit 10 Ridgewood Industrial Park,

Uckfield, East Sussex,

TN22 5QE England

Tel: +44 (0) 1825 749494

www.naval-military-press.com

www.nmarchive.com

This diary has been reprinted in facsimile from the original. Any imperfections are inevitably reproduced and the quality may fall short of modern type and cartographic standards.

© **Crown Copyright**
Images reproduced by permission of The National Archives, London, England, 2015.

Contents

Document type	Place/Title	Date From	Date To
Miscellaneous	8		
Heading	War Diary of 3rd Cavalry Division Intelligence Summaries March 1918		
Miscellaneous	Cover For Documents. Nature Of Enclosures.		
Miscellaneous	Narrative of Operations Carried Out By 3rd Cavalry Division		
Miscellaneous	Narrative of Operations of 3rd Dismounted Division		
Miscellaneous	Narrative of Operations of 6th Dismounted Brigade		
Miscellaneous	Action of 3rd Cavalry Division at Villeselve.		
Diagram etc	Diagram		
Miscellaneous	Narrative of Operations of Brigadier General Portal's Detachment		
Miscellaneous	Action Of Harman's Force		
Miscellaneous	Narrative of Operations-Canadian Cavalry Brigade		
Miscellaneous	3rd Cavalry Division Points Brought To Notice During Recent Operations		
Miscellaneous	Appendix "B"		
Miscellaneous	Not For Visitors		
Miscellaneous	Narrative of Operations Carried Out By 3rd Cavalry Division		
Miscellaneous	Narrative of Operations of 3rd Dismounted Division		
Miscellaneous	Narrative And Diary of Operations of 3rd Cavalry Division		
Miscellaneous	3rd Cavalry Division Narrative Of Operations	15/10/1918	15/10/1918
Miscellaneous	6th Cavalry Brigade Narrative of Operations	11/10/1918	11/10/1918
Miscellaneous	Narrative of Operations of 6th Dismounted Brigade		
Miscellaneous	Action Of 3rd Cavalry Division at Villeselve		
Diagram etc	Diagram		
Miscellaneous	Narrative of Operations of Brigadier General Portal's Detachment		
Miscellaneous	Action Of Harman's Force		
Miscellaneous	Narrative of Operations-Canadian Cavalry Brigade		
Miscellaneous	Canadian Cavalry Brigade Narrative of Operations for Period 8th. 10 th Oct 1918		
Heading	War Diary of 3rd Cavalry Division Intelligence Summaries May 1918		
Miscellaneous	Cover For Documents. Nature Of Enclosures.		
Miscellaneous	List Of Appendices		
Miscellaneous	A Form Messages And Signals		
Operation(al) Order(s)	3rd Cavalry Division Order No.28	03/05/1918	03/05/1918
Miscellaneous	March Table Issued With 3rd Cavalry Division Order No.28		
Miscellaneous	A Form Messages And Signals		
Operation(al) Order(s)	3rd Cavalry Division Order No.29	04/05/1918	04/05/1918
Miscellaneous	March Table Issued With 3rd Cavalry Division Order No.29		
Miscellaneous	Warning Order	04/05/1918	04/05/1918
Miscellaneous	III Corps Cavalry Corps	04/05/1918	04/05/1918
Miscellaneous	Appendix "A"		
Operation(al) Order(s)	3rd Cavalry Division Order No.30	05/05/1918	05/05/1918

Miscellaneous	March Table Issued With 3rd Cavalry Division Order No.30		
Miscellaneous	A Form Messages And Signals		
Miscellaneous	3rd Cavalry Division	05/05/1918	05/05/1918
Miscellaneous	A Form Messages And Signals		
Miscellaneous	3rd Cavalry Division	08/05/1918	08/05/1918
Miscellaneous	6th Cavalry Brigade	09/05/1918	09/05/1918
Miscellaneous	A Form Messages And Signals		
Miscellaneous	6th Cavalry Brigade	10/05/1918	10/05/1918
Operation(al) Order(s)	3rd Cavalry Division Order No.31	15/05/1918	15/05/1918
Miscellaneous	March Table Issued With 3rd Cavalry Division Order No.31		
Miscellaneous	A Form Messages And Signals		
Operation(al) Order(s)	3rd Cavalry Division Order No.32	22/05/1918	22/05/1918
Miscellaneous	March Table Issued With 3rd Cavalry Division Order No.32		
Operation(al) Order(s)	3rd Cavalry Division Order No.33	29/05/1918	29/05/1918
Miscellaneous	March Table Issued With 3rd Cavalry Division Order No.33		

Confidential

War Diary of

"A" Staff

3rd Cavalry Division

Intelligence Summaries.

March, 1918.

(6339) Wt. W160/M3016 1,500,000 10/17 McA & W Ltd (E 1898) Forms W3091.   Army Form W.3091.

Cover for Documents.

Nature of Enclosures.

Notes, or Letters written.

NARRATIVE OF OPERATIONS CARRIED OUT BY 3RD CAVALRY DIVISION

MARCH 21st to APRIL 5th, 1918.

March 21st.   At 8.0 a.m. the 3rd Cavalry Division received orders from Cavalry Corps to be ready to move at 2 hours notice.
   At 3.5. p.m. orders were received to move forthwith to an area about CUGNY coming under the orders of the III Corps. Divisional Headquarters were established at BEAUMONT-EN-BEINE. Brigades got into bivouac about 10 p.m.
   Dismounted brigades were formed and the 6th Dismounted Brigade under Lieut.Colonel BURT, D.S.O. marched mounted to

March 22nd.   UGNY arriving there about 3 a.m. on the 22nd.

   The Brigade proceeded thence by bus to OGNES where they came under the orders of the 58th Division.
   The 7th Dismounted Brigade, commanded by Lieut.Colonel E.PATERSON, I.S.O. Inniskilling Dragoons, and the Canadian Dismounted Brigade, commanded by Lieut.Colonel MACDONALD, D.S.O.,M.C., - both Brigades under the command of Brigadier General SEYMOUR, D.S.O. - marched mounted at 8 a.m. to VILLEQUIER-AUMONT and thence on foot to FRIERES CAMP, about 1 mile N.E. of VILLEQUIER AUMONT.
   The led horses of these Brigades and remainder of the Division marched to an area VARESNES, BRETIGNY, PONTOISE.
   Divisional Headquarters was established at VARESNES.
   The operations of General SEYMOUR'S Force (7th and Canadian Dismounted Brigades) from 22nd - 25th are given in Appendix I, and those of 6th Dismounted Brigade in Appendix II.

March 23rd.   At 9.50 a.m., March 23rd, the Division was notified by telephone that the Germans had broken through the line at HAM, and was ordered to turn out as many mounted men as possible.
   Orders were issued to Brigades to turn out 50 mounted men per regiment, the column to concentrate as soon as possible under Lieut.Colonel PATERSON, Canadian Brigade, at the cross-roads, BRETIGNY, and thence to proceed via GRANDRU to BUCHOIRE, III Corps H.Q.
   On reporting to III Corps H.Q. General HARMAN was ordered to take command of the mounted detachments of 2nd and 3rd Cavalry Divisions, also of Colonel THEOBALD'S Infantry, 600 strong, a Detachment of No.13 Balloon Company, consisting of 8 Lewis Guns and personnel, one lorry and one tender, and "O" Battery R.H.A. The whole force was to be known as HARMAN'S DETACHMENT with Headquarters at BERLANCOURT.
   By 1 P.M. HARMAN'S Detachment (less THEOBALD'S Infantry and "O" Battery) was concentrated in position of readiness at BERLANCOURT and Officers' patrols were sent out as follows:-
   BEAUMONT, to get touch with General GREENLY.
   BROUCHY - LAUCOURT - OLLEZY, to get touch with enemy.
   BERLANCOURT - MUILLE VILETTE - HAM, to get touch with enemy.
   ESMERY HALLON - CANIZY, to get touch with enemy.

   Strength of HARMAN'S Detachment was now approximately as follows:-

......2nd Cav.

March 23rd. (continued)	2nd Cav. Div. Mounted Detachment C.O. Capt. BONHAM.	... 300
	3rd Cav. Div. Mounted Detachment C.O. Lt.Col. PATERSON, D.S.O.	... 450 750 mounted men.
	THEOBALD'S Detachment C.O. Lt.Col. THEOBALD.	... ... 600 infantry.
	Detachment, No.13 Balloon Company, with 8 Lewis Guns.	... 38

"O" Battery R.H.A.

Light Section, 7th Cavalry Field Ambulance.

THEOBALD'S Infantry and "O" Battery R.H.A. joined at BERLANCOURT about 4.30 p.m. and shortly afterwards III Corps placed HARMAN'S Detachment at the disposal of General GREENLY, Commanding 14th Division.

At 6.45 p.m. orders were received from 14th Division to fill up a gap on the left of their support line from cross-roads 1000 yards E. of VILLESELVE Church to HILL 81. This order was cancelled 15 minutes later by a galloper from 14th Division, and 2nd and 3rd Cavalry Division Detachments were ordered instead to fill up a gap on the right of 14th Division line between VILLEQUIER AUMONT and LA NEUVILLE-EN-BEINE.

On proceeding to UGNY for this purpose, it was found that General SEYMOUR was already occupying this line with his dismounted force. Lt.Col. PATERSON telephoned to G.O.C. 14th Division and received instructions to bivouac the night at UGNY and return to BERLANCOURT early the next morning.

At 11 p.m. orders were received to send THEOBALD'S Infantry to block the Western exits of VILLESELVE which was done, Col. THEOBALD and No.13 Balloon Company taking up a position in a semi-circle on the Western side of, and about 300 yards from, VILLESELVE. "O" Battery was sent to a position N.E. of BERLANCOURT to cover VILLESELVE.

During the day, Divisional H.Q. Rear, all led horses and "B" Echelon moved to the CARLEPONT area under the command of Brigadier General PORTAL, D.S.O.

March 24th.   At 7.30 a.m. March 24th, 14th Division issued orders that 2nd and 3rd Cavalry Division Detachments of HARMAN'S Detachment were to be employed in protecting the left flank of 14th Division by filling a gap in the line from cross-roads 1000 yards E. of VILLESELVE Church to HILL 81. THEOBALD'S Infantry was to remain in position W. of VILLESELVE.

3rd Cavalry Division Detachment was sent to carry out this task with "O" Battery in position to support them.

2nd Cavalry Division Detachment was kept in reserve at BERLANCOURT.

At 11.10 a.m. a telephone message was received from III Corps ordering HARMAN'S Detachment to clear up the situation between ESMERY HALLON and GOLANCOURT. 2nd Cavalry Division Detachment was sent forward for this purpose

At 11.50 a.m. a message was received from 14th Division notifying their withdrawal through 9th French Division and ordering HARMAN'S Detachment to continue to protect the left flank of 9th French Division.

......A

-3-

March 24th.
(continued)
A Staff Officer reported to 9th French Division H.Q. 1.30 p.m. and received verbal orders to move the whole of HARMAN'S Detachment as rapidly as possible to BEAUGIES and take up a position between BEAUGIES and CREPIGNY to protect 9th French Division right flank.

This order could not be carried out because 2nd Cavalry Division Detachment was in action near ESMERY HALLON and 3rd Cavalry Division Detachment near VILLESELVE, and it was impossible to withdraw either force.

9th French Division were notified and said that as they could not have the cavalry they did not want THEOBALD'S Detachment which by now numbered about 400 only.

The order which had been sent to THEOBALD'S Detachment to concentrate at BERLANCOURT on first receipt of 9th French Division order was therefore cancelled, and they remained in position W. of VILLESELVE.

About 2.30 p.m. 3rd Cavalry Division Detachment came into action mounted N. of VILLESELVE. As a result of this action 100 prisoners were taken, about 100 enemy sabred, and the remains of 2 Battalions which were surrounded at CUGNY were enabled to extricate themselves. A full account of this action is given in Appendix III.

At 4.55 p.m. orders were issued to units of HARMAN'S Detachment to withdraw to GUISCARD, mounted troops covering the retirement of all infantry in the vicinity until GUISCARD was reached, and then to come into reserve at MUIRANCOURT.

Headquarters of the Detachment moved to MUIRANCOURT.

Those orders were duly carried out, except that 2nd Cavalry Division Detachment remained in neighbourhood of FRENICHES.

Under orders of III Corps, Lieut. Col. REYNOLDS, Commanding Northumberland Hussars, drew 120 horses from the led horses of the 3rd Cavalry Division during the night 24/25th and with the 120 men of his regiment thus mounted joined General HARMAN'S Force at 8 a.m.

March 25th.

Divisional H.Q. Rear with "B" Echelon and led horses moved to OLLENCOURT before noon. 650 led horses per Brigade were left at CARLEPONT for the dismounted Brigades of General SEYMOUR'S and Col. BURT'S Forces. The 7th and Canadian Brigades took over these horses during the afternoon. Owing to the tactical situation it was impossible to withdraw the 6th Dismounted Brigade from the line on the 25th.

At 1.50 a.m. March 25th, enemy were reported in close proximity to GUISCARD, and at 3.20 a.m., under orders issued by III Corps to General HARMAN personally, the Detachment less THEOBALD'S Infantry concentrated at LAGNY. Colonel THEOBALD'S Infantry was ordered to move to BEAURAINS and came under the orders of the Brigadier General there.

At 9.15 a.m. Colonel COOK'S Detachment of 2nd Cavalry Division, 500 strong, was placed under the orders of General HARMAN. They were, however, operating in the vicinity of BEAURAINS under 14th Division.

At 1.30 p.m. orders were received from the 14th Division to the effect that HARMAN'S Detachment would act under the orders of 10th French Division.

G.O.C. 10th French Division ordered HARMAN'S Detachment to act in co-operation with French Infantry Regimental Commander at CATIGNY. As a result of an interview with this Officer, the following dismounted party was ordered up to a reserve position immediately S.W. of MUIRANCOURT at 3 p.m.

......O.C.

-4-

March 25th.
(continued)

O.C. Col. PATERSON, D.S.O.

3rd Cavalry Division Party ... 350 men.
2nd   "   "   "   ... 250 "
                                 ─────
                                 600 "
                                 ═════

Col. COOK'S Detachment concentrated at LAGNY for this purpose and Col. COOK assumed command of 2nd Cavalry Division Detachment. At 6 p.m. Col. PATERSON reported the French to be retiring from MUIRANCOURT; he was consequently ordered to retire to his horses, mount and protect the retirement of the French Infantry.

This he did and then took up a line between the River and the main road from CATIGNY - SERMAIZE.

March 26th.

About 4 a.m. Brigadier General PORTAL received orders by telephone from Lieut. General BUTLER, Commanding III Corps, to collect a force of all available mounted men from CARLEPONT, OLLENCOURT and BAILLY (2nd Cav. Div. Details), and assemble as a Corps Reserve at LES CLOYES (P.20.). Strong patrols were to be sent to SEMPIGNY and PONTOISE and the enemy was to be prevented from crossing the River OISE. Communication was to be established with 18th Division at CAISNES and with General PITMAN, Commanding Mounted Detachment of 2nd Cavalry Division at CHIRY. In compliance with these orders a force consisting of 650 mounted men, together with 3rd Field Squadron R.E., was concentrated at LES CLOYES at 7.30 a.m. on the morning of 27th. The 7th and Canadian Brigade Detachments from CARLEPONT joined the force at 9.30 a.m. The narrative of the operations of this force is given in Appendix IV.

The remainder of Divisional H.Q. Rear with led horses and "B" Echelon divisionalized marched to CHOISY AU BAC just N. of COMPIEGNE. Brigades bivouacked along the N. edge of the FORET DE COMPIEGNE with "B" Echelons and Reserve Park in the forest. Divisional H.Q. Rear was established in CHOISY with General SEYMOUR in command.

At 3.30 a.m. March 26th, HARMAN'S Detachment withdrew through the French Infantry to reserve at DIVES, remaining under the orders of G.O.C. 10th French Division.

At 9.50 a.m. enemy were reported to have entered the BOIS DES ESSARTS. 2nd Cavalry Division Detachment were consequently ordered to move to the Fme. CHARBONNEAUX (Square I.1.b.) and take up a position running N.W. and S.E. through that place. 3rd Cavalry Division Detachment to BOIS DES CUBISTES in support and "O" Battery to North of BOIS DE LA RESERVE.

At 10.35 a.m. 3rd Cavalry Division Detachment was ordered to attack and occupy high ground in BOIS DES ESSARTS about I.9.central. Details of this action are given in Appendix V.

HARMAN'S Detachment then withdrew to THIESCOURT, reformed and then went into Reserve at ELINCOURT.

March 27th.

At 9 a.m. orders were received from III Corps for all details of 2nd Cavalry Division and Canadian Cavalry Brigade to move forthwith to VENETTE (W. of COMPIEGNE) where they would come under the orders of G.O.C. 2nd Cavalry Division.

.........The

-5-

March 27th.
(continued).
The remainder of HARMAN'S Detachment was placed under the orders of Lieut.Col. REYNOLDS (12th Lancers), Commanding Northumberland Hussars. This detachment, to be known as REYNOLDS Force, was composed as follows:-

	Officers.	O.R.
6th Cavalry Brigade Detachment.	5	89
7th " " "	4	125
Northumberland Hussars.	6	70
	15	284

together with 2 Vickers Guns from a M.M.G. Battery.

It was placed under the orders of General PERKINS, Commanding III Corps H.A., for reconnaissance work and was billeted at CHEVINCOURT.

"O" Battery was placed under the orders of 14th D.A.

During 27th, night 27/28th, 28th and night 28/29th this force was employed patrolling the line CHIRY - THIESCOURT - LASSIGNY - CANNY - BIERMONT.

This front was now held entirely by French troops supported by British Artillery. The information obtained by the patrols as to the position of the French and enemy forces was of great value to the British Artillery.

General HARMAN with his Staff rejoined the Division at CHOISY on the morning of the 27th. General PORTAL'S Force, less 1 Squadron of the Inniskilling Dragoons, arrived at CHOISY during the afternoon. Col. BURT'S Force (6th Dismounted Brigade) also rejoined.

The Division was therefore reconstituted with the following exceptions:-

(a) Canadian Cav. Bde. attached 2nd Cavalry Division.
(b) About 200 men of 6th and 7th Brigades with REYNOLDS Force.
(c) 1 Squadron Inniskilling Dragoons remaining in observation about LES CLOYES.

March 28th. Division remained at CHOISY.

March 29th. The Division marched North towards AMIENS, Divisional H.Q. for the night being situated at LES MESNIL-SUR-BULLES, (5 miles E. of ST.JUST-EN-CHAUSSEE).

The detachments of 3rd Cavalry Division from REYNOLDS Force and the squadron Inniskilling Dragoons rejoined the Division. "C" Battery remained with 14th D.A.

March 30th. The Division marched to SAINS-EN-AMIENOIS, "Q" Rear with A,2 and "B" Echelons to WAILLY.

March 31st. 3rd Cavalry Division (less Canadian Cavalry Brigade) situated in SAINS-EN-AMIENOIS Area.

3 P.M. Received Fifth Army No.G.292 ordering Division to be prepared to move at short notice and placing 3rd Cavalry Division under orders of XIX Corps.

7.30 P.M. XIX Corps Order No. G.316 received, ordering 3rd Cavalry Division to concentrate in vicinity of BOIS DE GENTELLES by 8 a.m. April 1st.

April 1st. This concentration was completed by 7.30 a.m. April 1st and Divisional Headquarters established at North end of BOVES.

........10.50 a.m.

April 1st. (continued)	10.50 a.m. Orders received to place one Brigade at disposal of G.O.C. 2nd Cavalry Division for use if required to retain ground gained that morning. 7th Brigade detailed. G.O.C. 7th Cavalry Brigade was already in touch with G.O.C. 2nd Cavalry Division.

The Inniskillings moved forward at 11 a.m. to HOURGES; the 7th Dragoon Guards at 1.30 p.m. to DOMART sur la LUCE. Both regiments came under orders of G.O.C. Canadian Cavalry Brigade (who was under orders of 2nd Cavalry Division) and were employed repelling counter-attack against RIFLE WOOD (C.10 and 11), and holding the Wood that night.

4.40 P.M. Received orders from XIX Corps for 3rd Cavalry Division, including troops detached, to concentrate that evening in Wood N.34.c., 2 miles N.W. of GENTELLES. 6th Cavalry Brigade and 3rd Field Squadron moved forthwith. 7th Cavalry Brigade completed their move, after having been relieved, at 6.45 a.m. April 2nd. |
| April 2nd. | 8.30 a.m. 3rd Field Squadron was placed at disposal of G.O.C. 18th Division for work on the CACHY Switch line.

9.30 a.m. State of readiness - Off saddled but prepared to move at half an hour's notice.

10.20 a.m. XIX Corps notified 3rd Cavalry Division that one Brigade might be placed at disposal of G.O.C. 1st Cavalry Division that night.

11.0 a.m. Canadian Brigade having come under orders of 3rd Cavalry Division was ordered to concentrate in the BOIS DE BOVES.

An account of the operations of the Canadian Brigade from March 29th to April 1st is given in Appendix VI.

2 p.m. 3rd Cavalry Division Report Centre moved to BLANGY TRONVILLE.

5.25 p.m. Orders from XIX Corps to place one Brigade at disposal of G.O.C. 1st Cavalry Division. 6th Cavalry Brigade detailed and employed as follows:- |
| April 3rd. | One Regiment digging posts during night of 2nd/3rd in the "P" Line. On completion of work Regiment bivouacked about O.27.

One Regiment moved to vicinity of FOUILLOY at 6 a.m. 3rd, to be in mobile reserve ready to move at half an hour's notice.

Remainder of Brigade moved to O.27 on morning of 3rd April. Brigade Headquarters to FOUILLOY at 7 a.m. 3rd.

8.20 p.m. Ordered to place 2 M.G.Squadrons (6th and 8th) at disposal of 14th Division from 10 a.m. 4th inst.

At 7 p.m. orders received from XIX Corps for 6th Brigade to remain in reserve to 14th Division after the relief of 1st Cavalry Division on night 3rd/4th. |
| April 4th. | 9.5. a.m. Telephone message received from G.O.C. 6th Cavalry Brigade to effect that 6th Cavalry Brigade had been ordered to fill gaps in 14th Division front. 10th Hussars ordered to fill the gap in centre of 14th Division on high ground about P.13. 3rd Dragoon Guards and Royals ordered to fill gap between 9th Australian Brigade and 14th Division.

9.10 a.m. 7th Cavalry Brigade ordered to saddle up and stand to at short notice.

9.15 a.m. Orders from XIX Corps for 7th Cavalry Brigade to move to a position of readiness about O.22 in support of 14th Division.

9.20 a.m. Canadian Cavalry Brigade ordered to saddle up and stand to in the BOIS DE BOVES. |

April 4th.
(continued).

About 12 Noon one Regiment (17th Lancers) 7th Cavalry Brigade sent forward to support Lieut.Col. BURT, Commanding 3rd Dragoon Guards and Royals on 14th Division right.

12.25 p.m. Advanced Divisional Report Centre established at 14th Division Headquarters, FOUILLOY.

1.37 p.m. 7th Cavalry Brigade ordered to send one Regiment (7th Dragoon Guards) to reinforce 10th Hussars and Infantry in the line from P.20.a.0.8. to VAIRE-SOUS-CORBIE.

Situation at 1 p.m. was:-

9th Australian Brigade ...	from V.2.a. - cottages in P.25.c.
3rd Dragoon Guards and Royals.) ...	Cottages P.25.c. - P.19.b.2.3.
Infantry of 14th Divn. ...	P.19.b.2.3. - P.13.b.5.0.
10th Hussars.	P.13.b.5.0. - P.8.central.
Infantry of 14th Divn. ...	P.8.central to VAIRE-SOUS-CORBIE.

17th Lancers in support of 3rd Dragoon Guards and Royals.

7th Dragoon Guards about to be sent to reinforce 10th Hussars.

About 2 p.m. Lieut.Col.BURT, Commanding 3rd Dragoon Guards and Royals reported that he had the situation well in hand.

At 4.30 p.m. Brigadier General A.E.W.HARMAN, D.S.O., Commanding 3rd Cavalry Division, received orders by telephone from XIX Corps to take over command of the Left Sector from Major General SKINNER, Commanding 14th Divn.

At 5 p.m. 15th Australian Brigade was placed at the disposal of G.O.C. 3rd Cavalry Division. Two Battalions of this Brigade had already been moved to reinforce the left of the 14th Division about VAIRE-SOUS-CORBIE.

At 8 p.m. 15th Australian Brigade was ordered to take over the line from the WARFUSEE ABANCOURT - FOUILLOY road to the SOMME, relieving units of the 14th Division, the 10th Hussars and the 7th Dragoon Guards then in that line, and the 6th Cavalry Brigade to take over the line from ST.QUENTIN - AMIENS road (inclusive) at P.25.c.8.2. to the WARFUSEE ABANCOURT - FOUILLOY road (exclusive) at P.20.a.0.9.

This relief was completed at 5 a.m. April 5th and all units of the 7th Cavalry Brigade placed under the orders of G.O.C. 6th Cavalry Brigade.

The 43rd Infantry Brigade on relief remained in reserve under orders of G.O.C. 3rd Cavalry Division concentrated about O.24.a.

The 11th Kings, under orders of G.O.C. 43rd Infantry Brigade, were ordered to dig and occupy a line of posts from about O.30.central - O.24.d.central - O.18.d.central.

All M.Gs. remained in the line. They consisted of the following:-

M.Gs. of 1st Cavalry Division.
" " 3rd "
16th Machine Gun Battalion.
14th

.....16th D.A.

April 4th.
(continued)

16th Divisional Artillery continued to cover front taken over by 3rd Cavalry Division.

Led horses of 3rd Cavalry Division were moved back to N.34.c.

The Canadian Cavalry Brigade in the BOIS DE BOVES had been ordered to off-saddle at 5.10 p.m.

The night of 4/5th was uneventful.

April 5th.

At 11 a.m. on the 5th, the enemy attacked on the whole Divisional front after an intense bombardment of 45 minutes duration.

6th Cavalry Brigade and 15th Australian Infantry Brigade reported attack was stopped dead by M.G. and Artillery fire.

15th Australian Infantry reported repulse of attack by telephone.

6th Cavalry Brigade reported as follows:-

"G.B.156. 5th. Timed 1.10 p.m.

Lt.Col. BURT reports the whole of his front has been bombarded heavily. His casualties are very small AAA Strong attack developed on his whole front about 11 a.m. This attack was stopped dead by M.G. and Arty. AAA Enemy forming up again about 12.45 p.m. AAA Col. BURT reports he is strongly dug in and is confident of being able to deal with the situation AAA 7th Cavalry Brigade equally happy AAA Ends."

The Artillery were informed of massing of enemy referred to in 6th Cavalry Brigade report. No attack developed.

At 3 p.m. 5th Australian Division was ordered to relieve 3rd Cavalry Division in Left Sector.

The relief was completed uneventfully at 4 a.m. April 6th, and 3rd Cavalry Division moved to C.MON area on the 6th and came into III Corps Reserve, and subsequently rejoined Cavalry Corps.

APPENDIX I.

Narrative of Operations of 3rd Dismounted Division.

March 22nd - 25th, 1918.

March 22nd. Headquarters, 6th Cavalry Brigade formed Headquarters, 3rd Dismounted Division at 7 a.m. 22nd March, and established their Headquarters at VILLEQUIER AUMONT.

6th Dismounted Brigade moved by bus at 1 a.m. to OGNES, on arrival there to come under the orders of 58th Division.

7th and Canadian Dismounted Brigades were encamped in the Wood in huts at S.14.central FRIERES Wood, by 10 a.m. with 8th and Canadian Machine Gun Squadrons, 8 and 12 machine guns respectively.

The 3rd Dismounted Division were in III Corps Reserve.

Owing to uncertainty of situation about TERGNIER, 7th Dismounted Brigade were placed under orders of 18th Divn., and 35 busses were sent to be ready to move them about 2.30 p.m., but 7th Dismounted Brigade only 'Stood To' at ½ hours notice.

H.Q. and Canadian Dismounted Brigade were to remain in III Corps Reserve.

2.30 p.m. Message received from G.O.C. III Corps that it was his intention to prevent the enemy crossing the CROZAT Canal, and that in consequence various adjustments between the 14th, 18th and 58th Divisional Sectors would take place. The 3rd, 4th, and 5th Cavalry Dismounted Brigades were put at the disposal of the 14th Division. 6th Dismounted Brigade was to remain at disposal of 58th Division The 7th Cavalry Dismounted Brigade was to be at the disposal of 18th Division and the Canadian Cavalry Dismtd. Brigade to remain in Corps Reserve in FRIERES Wood.

3.5 p.m. 7th Dismounted Brigade ordered to prepare to embuss, under orders of 18th Division. 35 busses arrived. General LEE (G.O.C. 18th Division) and G.O.C. 3rd Dismounted Division went to FRIERES Wood, where they sited 6 Machine Guns of 7th Dismounted Brigade.

3.45 p.m. Canadian Dismounted Brigade placed at disposal of 18th Division and ordered to send Officers to reconnoitre routes to VOUEL (T.19.c.).

8.15 p.m. 7th Dismounted Brigade ordered to occupy defences on the Eastern edge of FRIERES Wood from the PHEASANTRY Southwards for about 1000 yards.

9.55 p.m. 18th Division ordered half of Canadian Dismounted Brigade to be placed at the disposal of General SADLEIR JACKSON (G.O.C. 54th Infantry Brigade) as a Reserve (not to be used in counter-attack). One section of Machine Gun Squadron to accompany.

11 p.m. 7th Dismounted Brigade in position as ordered, with 7th Dragoon Guards on the right and in touch with the Queens, 17th Lancers on the left, and in touch with East Surreys, and Inniskilling Dragoons in reserve on main road S.15.b.9.0.

March 23rd. 2.45 a.m. Canadian Dismounted Brigade report 4 machine guns being sent to 54th Brigade.

9.0 a.m. One regiment Canadian Dismounted Brigade moved to 54th Brigade.

8.30 a.m. Whole of the Canadian Dismounted Brigade, under orders of 18th Division, were placed at the disposal of 54th Brigade.

11.30 a.m. Two Squadrons Inniskilling Dragoons sent to reinforce 7th Dragoon Guards.

12.15 p.m. 7th Dismounted Brigade report that troops

........on

Appendix I (continued).

March 23rd. on their right were gradually retiring, both French and
(continued) British, and they were being forced to prolong their right
to conform. The 3rd Squadron Inniskilling Dragoons was
consequently sent to the right to form a Defensive Flank.
    12.30 p.m. 7th Dismounted Brigade placed at disposal
of G.O.C. 55th Brigade.
    1 p.m. Under orders of 18th Division, the 3rd
Dismounted Division moved to UGNY. The 6th Cavalry Field
Ambulance remained at VILLEQUIER AUMONT, sending one Medical
Officer and one Ambulance each to the 7th and Canadian
Dismounted Brigades.
    6 p.m. Owing to news being received that the Germans
were getting round VILLEQUIER AUMONT from the N.W. and were
approaching UGNY from the woods to the North, the G.O.C. 3rd
Dismounted Division was ordered by G.O.C. 18th Division to
assume command of details then in UGNY, and to take up a
position on the high ground to the N.E. of the village
overlooking GUYENCOURT.
    By 6.30 p.m. about 2,000 men consisting of 600 men 2nd
Cavalry Division, Entrenching Battalions and Infantry
Details, with Machine Guns, were in position, and began to
dig themselves in. The 7th Dismounted Brigade, having been
relieved by the French, here rejoined the Division. At
9.30 p.m. the 1st French Dismounted Cavalry Division and
the 9th French Infantry Division had passed through and
taken up a position near VILLEQUIER AUMONT. The force under
General SEYMOUR then withdrew.

    The Canadian Dismounted Brigade rejoined about 10 p.m.
and bivouacked in the BOIS CAUMONT.

March 24th. Infantry details were handed over to A.P.M. 18th Divn.,
at CAILLOUEL, for despatch to their unit.
    The 3rd Dismounted Division with about 600 other ranks
of 2nd Dismounted Division marched to CAILLOUEL, where they
camped for three hours. Owing to the continuance of the
German advance, the 18th Division wished to clear the
village to facilitate the passage of heavy artillery. The
3rd Dismounted Division and 2nd Cavalry Division details
consequently marched to bivouac immediately West of
DAMPCOURT.
    4 p.m. General SEELY assumed command of 2nd and 3rd
Dismounted Divisions, with Headquarters at APPILLY, and at
the same time the Dismounted Cavalry came under the orders
of General DIBOLD, Commanding 125th French Infantry Divn.
    DAMPCOURT and the bivouac were shelled between 6 and 7
p.m.
    Posts were put out between the OISE Canal and the
NOYON-CHAUNY Road.

March 25th. 4 a.m. The 2nd Cavalry Division details were withdrawn
to their horses and went to VARESNES, where they rejoined
their own Division.
    4.15 a.m. Owing to the enemy forcing back the French,
the 3rd Dismounted Division was ordered to take up a
defensive position round APPILLY to cover their retirement.
    9.0 a.m. The following were the dispositions:-
    1 Squadron Lord Strathcona's Horse was in MONDESCOURT.
The 17th Lancers and Inniskilling Dragoons held a line
from the X-roads NOYON - CHAUNY - CREPIGNY - DAMPCOURT to
the Canal, with 7th Dragoon Guards thrown back to form a
defensive flank to the South. The Royal Canadian Dragoons
were at PETIT QUIERCY where they had been sent to help
Colonel PICHAT, and 5 Squadrons were in reserve at the
Chateau at APPILLY.

Appendix I (continued)

March 25th. 11-0.am. under orders of the III Corps, all the
(continued) Cavalry were withdrawn from the line, concentrated at
BRETIGNY, and marched back independently to their horses
at CARLEPONT. The enemy occupied APPILLY about 1-30.pm.,
crossed the Canal, and took up a position north of the
OISE, the French holding the line of the River.

-x-x-x-x-x-x-x-x :-: x-x-x-x-

APPENDIX II.

Narrative of Operations of 6th Dismounted Brigade.

March 21st - 27th, 1918.

March 21st. Left DEVISE 4.45 p.m. 3rd Cavalry Division marched to BEAUMONT (30 miles).

March 22nd. At 2 a.m. 6th Dismounted Brigade was formed, under Lieut. Colonel A. BURT, D.S.O., 3rd Dragoon Guards.
Strength:
- 3rd Dragoon Guards ... 180)
- 1st Royal Dragoons ... 180) approximately.
- 10th Royal Hussars ... 120)
- 6th M.G. Squadron ... 60)

and proceeded by bus from UGNY to VIRY NOUREUIL, arriving at 4.30 a.m., coming under orders of 173rd Infantry Brigade (Brig. General MORGAN, 58th Division).
A trench line partly dug, was taken up between VIRY NOUREUIL and NOUREUIL. Headquarters at NOUREUIL. 3rd Dragoon Guards on right with 14th Pioneer Battalion on South Flank; Royals in centre and 10th Hussars on left, with a Detachment of 3rd LONDON Regiment and 14th Division (BEDFORD Regiment) on their left.
Day spent in improving trenches and putting up wire.

March 23rd. Following on a counter-attack made by 133rd French Regiment on TERGNIER and the BUTTS, the Germans delivered a fresh attack which overwhelmed the counter-attack and broke through in masses at the BUTTS. Another force broke through further North and rapidly arrived at N.N.E. entrance of NOUREUIL on our extreme left flank. The Cavalry Line, which was attacked twice in various parts, maintained its position, and Officers of the 2nd and 3rd LONDON Regiment and 6th Dismounted Brigade Headquarters rallied troops falling back, throwing out a defensive flank and holding on to the village till dark.

March 24th. The 6th Dismounted Brigade received orders from the 58th Division to withdraw to a line about CHAUNY. This was done without incident, although the Germans were only 100 yards distant in the outskirts of the village and to the West of it. At 5.30 a.m. a line was taken up in the Sunk road running North from CHAUNY with details of the LONDON Regt. and Oxford Hussars on the right and French troops (133rd) on left. Germans attacked at 8.30 a.m. under cover of mist. They advanced up to 20 yards, speaking English, and were driven back by Hotchkiss and Rifle fire. About 9.30 a.m. the mist lifted, and it was found that the French had moved back. The order was received to move to ABBECOURT. This had to be done over open country, under very heavy machine gun fire, as the Germans had advanced round CHAUNY on the right and forced the French back on the left.
The night was spent at MANICAMP lining the Canal.

March 25th. At 9.30 a.m., ordered by Colonel Commanding French Divn. (Colonel PICHAT) to move to high ground South of QUIERZY. To carry out this movement, an Officer was sent to the head of the Column and directed it to a position immediately outside QUIERZY, where it came under heavy shell fire.
The Column therefore moved across the open to a position at LES BRUYERES.
At about 12 Noon, an order was received from the Brigade (173rd) to re-occupy QUIERZY, and at the same time instructions

........were

Appendix II (continued).

March 25th. (continued) were received only to take orders from our own Brigadier. Units in this area had been at first placed under orders of the French, but dual control had started, and the scheme proved unworkable.

QUIERZY was occupied by half the Dismounted Brigade, the remainder being held in Reserve.

The bridges over the Canal had been blown up, and the one over the River was burning.

March 26th. Relieved by LONDON Regiments and marched to BESME, arriving there at 6 a.m. The Brigadier, 173rd Infantry Brigade expressed his satisfaction at the way the work had been carried out.

At 3 p.m. marched to TRACY-LE-MONT, on the way being inspected by Major General CATOR (G.O.C. 58th Division) who issued a letter expressing his great appreciation of the work carried out by the 6th Dismounted Brigade.

March 27th. At 11 a.m. horses were sent to meet the 6th Dismounted Brigade, which broke up and joined their respective units at CROISY-AU-BAC.

-x-x-x-x-x-x-x-x-x-x-

APPENDIX III.

Action of 3rd Cavalry Division at VILLESELVE.

At 8.30 a.m. 24th March, received orders at BERLANCOURT to push forward in the direction of CUGNY in support of disorganized infantry. On reaching VILLESELVE Infantry line had broken. Cavalry was pushed forward and line re-established from BEAUMONT to neighbourhood of EAUCOURT. Were ordered to withdraw to support the 9th French Division but Infantry line again broke on withdrawal of Cavalry. General HARMAN issued orders to return to restore situation. The 7th and Canadian Brigades were sent mounted around the Southern side of VILLESELVE and established a line from BEAUMONT, which was the left of the French position, to the road junction ½ mile N.W. of BEAULIEU. The 6th Brigade under Major WILLIAMS was sent through COLLEZY with instructions to charge through the German line, then swing right handed in a N.E. direction along their line, using the sword only.

The Detachment moved along the main road to VILLESELVE, taking the Sunken Track running North into COLLEZY. On approaching COLLEZY, it came under M.G. fire from direction of GOLANCOURT, but got under cover of a big farm at S.E. exit of village.

The Detachment was formed into 3 troops by regiments, 3rd Dragoon Guards under Lieut. VINCENT forming 1st wave, 10th Hussars under Major WILLIAMS 2nd wave, Royals under Capt. TURNER 3rd wave.

The attack was carried out in "Infantry Attack" formation, the first 2 waves in line extended, the 3rd in sections but covering the flanks of 2 leading waves.

The 3rd Dragoon Guards moved in the direction of COPSE A, encountering some German infantry who were either killed or captured. Some of the enemy ran into the Copse where they were followed on foot and many shot at point blank range in the back as they ran away. 12 prisoners were handed over to the Infantry by 3rd Dragoon Guards.

Major WILLIAMS led the 10th Hussars and Royals on the West side of COPSE A, where the greater part of the hostile infantry were posted. All three regiments were under M.G. fire for about 1000 yards (the last 200 yards was over plough), but when within 200 yards of the enemy, the latter, hearing the men cheering, surrendered freely. The 10th Hussars rode straight through the enemy. The Royals followed and mopped up small parties who had run together after the 10th had passed through them.

After the melee, "Rally" was sounded, prisoners collected, wounded picked up, and the Squadron returned to the main BERLANCOURT - VILLESELVE road. 94 prisoners were brought in by 10th Hussars and Royals, making a total of 106 in all. One M.G. was brought back intact and two others put out of action.

Besides the 106 prisoners taken, between 70 and 100 of the enemy were sabred. The losses of the Detachment were 73 out of 150, but the manoeuvre gave the Infantry renewed confidence and they pushed forward to a line running from the outskirts of GOLANCOURT almost to EAUCOURT, including HILL 81. This re-establishment enabled the remnants of 2 Battalions which had been fighting near CUGNY to retire on VILLESELVE, at which point they were re-assembled and sent back into the line.

.....French

Appendix III (continued)

French troops came up and the mounted detachment of the 3rd Cavalry Division withdrew to a support line across the main road ¾ mile S.W. of VILLESELVE. Orders were then received that the French having decided to take up a new line near GUISCARD the Cavalry was to cover the retirement of the Infantry to that point and then withdrew to MUIRANCOURT. This was done successfully.

-x-x-x-x-x-x-x-x-x-x-x-x-x-

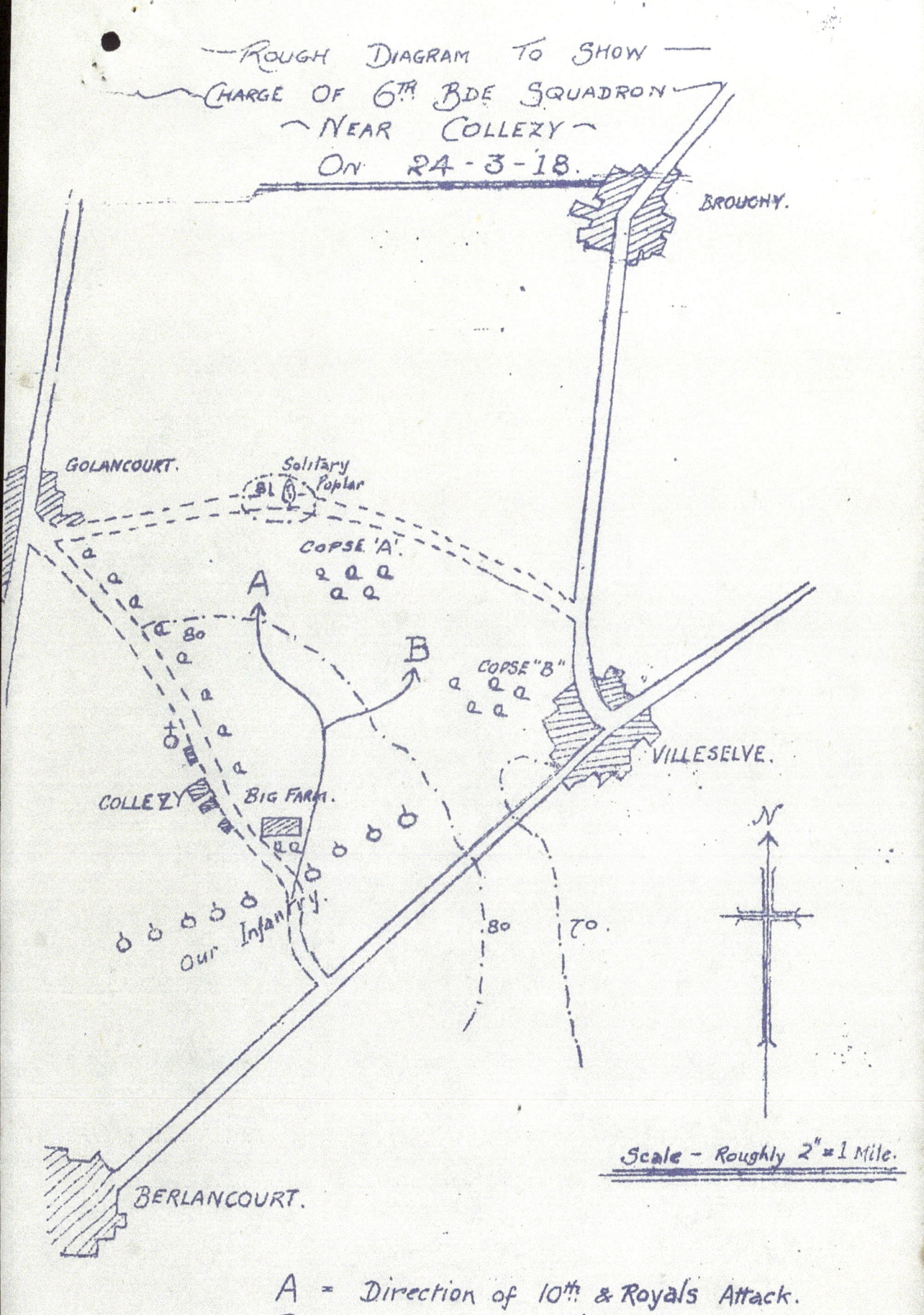

APPENDIX IV.

Narrative of Operations of Brigadier General PORTAL'S Detachment, March 26th - 27th.

March 26th.

7.30 a.m. Details of 3rd Cavalry Division, consisting of 650 other ranks and 3rd Field Squadron R.E., concentrated at Les CLOYES. 1 patrol of 100 other ranks 7th Cavalry Brigade was sent to PONTOISE, and 1 patrol of 100 other ranks Canadian Cavalry Brigade to SEMPIGNY, to remain in observation at those places. Standing patrol (6 O.R.) sent to OURSCAMP. Liaison Officers sent to 18th Division at CAISNES and to 2nd Cavalry Division at CHIRY.

9.0 a.m. Patrols reported:-

(a) French Dismounted Cavalry holding the front line from BRETIGNY - PONTOISE. Both bridges at VARESNES destroyed. Those at PONTOISE prepared for demolition.

(b) Enemy advancing on NOYON - SEMPIGNY Road, 2 kms. North of Canal. French troops holding SEMPIGNY. Bridge over the Canal prepared for demolition.

9.20 a.m. Bridges over OISE and Canal at SEMPIGNY reported destroyed. French troops holding S. bank of Canal VARESNES to MT. RENAUD.

9.30 a.m. 3rd Dismounted Division (less 6th Dismounted Brigade) joined the Detachment mounted.

10.15 a.m. Detachment ordered to move via OURSCAMP to support 2nd Cavalry Division in attack on high ground in I.22.b., 16.b., 10.a. (Sheet 70 E.).

11.0 a.m. Above order cancelled, Detachment to remain in Corps Reserve.

1.40 p.m. Right patrol reported that French had withdrawn to South Bank of River OISE and partially blown up bridges at PONTOISE.

2.35 p.m. Left patrol reported enemy attack developing against French at MT. RENAUD. Situation at SEMPIGNY quiet.

March 27th.

9.0 a.m. Morning report - situation quiet. Received orders for Canadian Cavalry Brigade to move with 2nd Cavalry Division to Fifth Army area.

11.0 a.m. Received orders for remainder of Detachment (less 1 Squadron) to concentrate at CHOISY. "B" Squadron Inniskilling Dragoons left at LES CLOYES as contact squadron to protect left flank of 18th Division and keep III Corps informed of the situation.

-x-x-x-x-x-x-x-x-x-

APPENDIX V.

Action of HARMAN'S FORCE.

March 26th - BOIS DES ESSARTS.

On the 26th, orders were received for the 3rd Cavalry Division Detachment to push the enemy out of the BOIS DES ESSARTS and Mt. De PORQUERICOURT in I.9.central where they had obtained a footing, and connect up from Fme. CHARBONNEAUX in I.1.b. to PITMAN'S Force in the neighbourhood of DIVES LE FRANC. This was done successfully, the attack being made by the Canadian Brigade and a portion of the 7th Cavalry Brigade dismounted, the remainder of the 6th and 7th Cavalry Brigades protecting the right flank by holding the BOIS DE LA RESERVE. Touch was obtained with PITMAN'S Force at road junction in I.15.central and with the 2nd Cavalry Division at edge of BOIS DES ESSARTS in I.2.d., thus establishing a line from North of DIVES LE FRANC to LAGNY. After connecting with PITMAN'S Force, the 6th Cavalry Brigade were withdrawn to a position in support in the neighbourhood of Detachment Headquarters at the Chateau in I.13.b.9.7. and direct communication was opened along the main road through GUY to HARMAN'S Detachment at DIVES.

The Northumberland Hussars which had been attached to the Canadian Brigade were detached to come under the command of Colonel COOK, 2nd Cavalry Division, and hold the high ground at Eastern end of Montagne De LAGNY. Later, the enemy, who had crossed at CATIGNY, broke through the French line in the neighbourhood of CANDON and turned the left flank of the 2nd Cavalry Division who were compelled to retire on DIVES. Col. COOK was killed at this time.

This left the left flank of the 3rd Cavalry Mounted Detachment exposed at the edge of the Wood in I.2.d.

The 6th Cavalry Brigade Detachment were ordered to push forward mounted in the direction of Fme. CHARBONNEAUX to support the 2nd Cavalry Division and were the last troops to withdraw. Colonel STEVENSON of the Canadian Brigade was sent to draw back the left flank in the BOIS DES ESSARTS, and all horses of the 3rd Cavalry Detachment were sent back through GUY under Captain PARBURY of the 17th Lancers.

Word was passed to PITMAN'S Force of the situation and that the 3rd Cavalry Division Detachment would protect his left flank. The latter fought a rearguard action on foot, gradually retiring on GUY, at which point a determined stand was made which delayed the enemy sufficiently to enable the 6th Cavalry Brigade Detachment to get clear and PITMAN'S Force to withdraw on DIVES LE FRANC. This action was continued over the BOIS DE LA RESERVE and BOIS DE CLOCHETTES, the 3rd Cavalry Detachment ultimately crossing the river at EVRICOURT and H.23.b.7.0., where the horses were waiting and where the French had put a line along the river. At this point orders were received to retire to ELINCOURT which was reached about 10 p.m. on the 26th.

-x-x-x-x-x-x-x-x-x-

APPENDIX VI.

Narrative of Operations - Canadian Cavalry Brigade.

(A) Capture of BOIS DE MOREUIL - March 30th.

(B) Capture of RIFLE WOOD   - April 1st.

A.

At 2 p.m. on March 29th, the Canadian Cavalry Brigade received orders to march to JUMEL. During the march orders were received to proceed to GUYENCOURT, where the Brigade bivouacked in GUYENCOURT Wood. The Brigade stood to at dawn on March 30th, having received orders at 2 a.m. to be ready to move at 6.30 a.m. The hour to move was postponed until 8.30 a.m. at which hour the G.O.C. met General PITMAN, Commanding 2nd Cavalry Division, who gave him the following information and orders.

The Germans had captured MEZIERES and were advancing rapidly towards AMIENS. The Brigade was to cross the NOYE and the AVRE Rivers as quickly as possible and engage and delay the enemy.

Orders were issued accordingly to move at once across country from REMIENCOURT, leaving BOIS LE SENCAT on the right, and endeavour to force a crossing at CASTEL. The crossing at CASTEL was unopposed and the Brigade proceeded due East to the Northern extremity of the BOIS DE MOREUIL. At that point considerable machine gun and rifle fire was encountered coming from the Northern face of the Wood. It was apparent that the retention of this Wood by the enemy, giving them direct observation on the whole of the Valley leading up to AMIENS, might be fatal to AMIENS, and the G.O.C. accordingly decided to attack and take the Wood.

Headquarters were established at the Northern edge of the small wood adjoining the large one. This small wood had not yet been occupied by the enemy. The Royal Canadian Dragoons, who were leading, were ordered to send an advance-guard Squadron, commanded by Capt. NORDHEIMER, at a gallop to clear the North-Western corner of the Wood, the 2nd Squadron, commanded by Capt. NEWCOMEN, also mounted, to the S.W. face of the Wood, with the object, if possible, of gaining touch with Major TIMMIS's Squadron at the extreme Southern corner of the Wood. The 3rd Squadron, commanded by Major TIMMIS, was ordered to gallop round the N.E. corner of the Wood up to the Southern corner. Capt. NORDHEIMER'S Squadron, although exposed to very heavy rifle and machine gun fire, passed through into the N.W. corner of the Wood and established themselves in the Wood, being joined later by Lord Strathcona's Horse. Capt. NEWCOMEN'S Squadron penetrated about half way up the S.W. face of the Wood, where they found heavy machine gun fire directed on them from the enemy, between MORISEL and MOREUIL. They turned into the Wood and established themselves there. Major TIMMIS's Squadron met with considerable opposition and wheeled to the left, suffering very heavy casualties.

Lord Strathcona's Horse (R.C.) were then ordered to send one Squadron under Lieut. FLOWERDEW to pass round the N.E. corner of the Wood at a gallop in support of Capt. NORDHEIMER, while the remaining two Squadrons of the Regiment advanced to the attack dismounted on the North-Western face. Capt. NORDHEIMER'S Squadron got into the Wood and engaged the enemy in hand-to-hand combat. Many of the enemy were killed, all refusing to surrender, but a large party, estimated about 300, retired from the Wood S.E. of the point where Capt. NORDHEIMER'S Squadron had entered it. This party were charged by Lieut. FLOWERDEW (Lord Strathcona's Horse) and many of the Germans were killed with the sword as they ran to meet the Cavalry with the bayonet, shewing no signs of surrender. Lieut. FLOWERDEW, having passed through them, wheeled about and charged again. He then galloped into the Wood at the centre of the Eastern face, established himself and was joined by the Dismounted party of his Regiment. Fierce hand-to-hand fighting ensued in all the N.E.

Appendix VI (continued)

part of the Wood, resulting ultimately in the complete capture of this portion of the Wood and the killing of all the German Garrison. The resistance of the enemy was most stubborn; one badly wounded German, shot through both legs and the stomach, refused to allow the Stretcher Bearers to move him, saying he would sooner die uncaptured. Meantime, Captain NEWCOMEN'S Squadron were held up half way down the Western face of the Wood, and the enemy still held out in some strength in the S. point of the Wood. Two Squadrons of Fort Garry Horse were sent to reinforce Capt. NEWCOMEN, and a 3rd Squadron of the same Regiment was sent across the River to enfilade the enemy from the high ground above MORISEL.

On the Northern face, 2 Squadrons of Lord Strathcona's Horse (R.C.) advanced dismounted, commanded by Lieut.Col. McDONALD. Many casualties were sustained in this advance, and no doubt the whole party would have been destroyed had it not been for the simultaneous attacks on the enemy's rear, of which he aware from the continuous rifle and machine gun fire. Lieut.Col. McDONALD'S Party entered the Wood and overcame all enemy resistance and by 11 a.m. the attack having started at 9.30 a.m., the whole Wood except the extreme Southern point was in possession of the Canadian Cavalry Brigade. The losses were severe, most Regiments having lost from half to one third of their Officers, and a similar proportion of their men, and it would have been impossible to have held the Wood but for the prompt arrival of General BELL-SMYTHE'S Brigade, who reinforced our weak points and bore the brunt of the fierce fighting later in the day in the Wood. In spite of repeated counter-attacks by the enemy the Wood was held by the Cavalry until 2.30 a.m. the following day, March 31st, when General SEELY handed over the defence of the captured wood, of which he had been placed in charge, to the Infantry of the 8th Division. On relief the Brigade retired and bivouacked in BOIS DE SENCAT, the Brigade H.Q. being established at CASTEL.

Throughout March 31st, the Brigade stood to near BOIS DE SENCAT, ready to assist the defence in case of counter-attack, but were not called upon.

D.

At 9.30 p.m. March 31st, orders were received from the 2nd Cavalry Division, to which the Canadian Cavalry Brigade were still attached, that the Division would counter-attack at dawn the following day. The G.O.C. and Brigade Major rode to GENTELLES and attended a Conference lasting from 2 a.m. to 4 a.m. on April 1st, planning the attack. The attack was to be made on RIFLE WOOD, one mile S. of HANGARD, which had been captured by the Germans. The command of the attacking forces, composed of the whole of the dismounted men of the 2nd Cavalry Division, was given to the G.O.C. Canadian Cavalry Brigade. The orders were drawn up and issued at 4 a.m.   and Commanding Officers of all units were ordered to meet General SEELY at DOMMARTIN at 7 a.m. The 4th Cavalry Brigade were ordered to lead the attack on the road running due S. from the Ridge at the N.E. corner of the Wood to HANGARD. The 5th Cavalry Brigade to seize the N.E. edge of the Wood, and the Canadian Cavalry Brigade to pass through the 5th Cavalry Brigade, and clear and occupy the Wood. During this operation the Canadian Cavalry Brigade was commanded by Lieut. Col. PATERSON, D.S.O.

The operation was covered by all available Artillery firing on laid down barrages, and also by concentrated machine gun fire from the 3 Machine Gun Squadrons. The Canadian Machine Gun Squadron was allotted the task of firing on the N.E. face of the Wood up to the last minute and then gradually switching through the Wood. These guns carried out this difficult operation most effectively.

....The attack

Appendix VI (continued).

The attack started at 9 a.m. and was completely successful, although the losses were heavy. The whole of the Wood was in our possession of 11 a.m. There was much fierce fighting, but the enemy shewed more willingness to surrender than on March 30th. Over 100 prisoners were taken and 13 Machine Guns. Of these 13 Machine Guns, 11 were used by the Hotchkiss gunners of the Canadian Cavalry Brigade against the enemy throughout the day.

The positions round the Wood were consolidated with the assistance of the 2nd Cavalry Division Field Squadron, Commanded by Major SWINBURN, who was killed while directing those operations. The enemy organized a strong counter-attack of a whole Brigade, marching from VILLERS AUX ERABLES; they were observed concentrating by our airmen. Meantime the road and Wood were very heavily shelled and the Oxfordshire Hussars and the 3rd Hussars on the left, and the 5th Cavalry Brigade and the Canadian Cavalry Brigade suffered somewhat severely. Reinforcements were asked for. The Inniskilling Dragoons were sent forward to the Wood and the Royal Scots Greys prolonged the flank from the Wood in the direction of THIENNES. The German counter-attack, when launched, was completely repulsed, and their losses were very severe, many hundreds of dead being left lying to the East and South of the Wood.

The Canadian Brigade was relieved at 6 p.m. and marched to the BOIS DE SENCAT.

3rd Cavalry Division.

Points brought to notice during recent Operations.

I. DISMOUNTED ACTION.

1. On arrival in the III Corps area, this division was ordered to form a Dismounted Division to go forward to occupy certain points of the defensive line. In the subsequent retirements which took place, difficulty was experienced in carrying equipment, rations, ammunition, coats warm British, etc., owing to the unsuitability of the kit of the Cavalry soldier for acting for prolonged periods dismounted; hence some equipment had to be abandoned. The horses on this occasion were sent back some miles under orders of the Corps and were not seen again by the units for 3 or 4 days. It has been brought out time after time during the operations that the horses must be kept within reasonable reach of the dismounted men, otherwise the latter lose a great deal of their mobility.

Mounted men must always be attached to a Dismounted Brigade for use as orderlies, patrol purposes, etc., and a mounted reserve kept in hand for counter-attack or moving quickly to a threatened point even when the remainder of the units are acting dismounted.

2. Pack horses for Hotchkiss, Machine Guns and tools and ammunition, led by men on foot, should always accompany the Dismounted Brigade or Regiment if it is found that the remainder of the horses must for tactical reasons be sent some distance away. Otherwise men are used up in carrying the above equipment.

3. It was found that when the Cavalry was sent forward to take up a position to check the enemy, or to fill up a gap which had occurred in the line, the situation was very obscure and it was very necessary to send officer's patrols forward at once to see the situation.

4. In retiring from one position to another it was found advisable to retire by a flank to avoid hostile artillery fire.

Previous reconnaissance of the next position it is proposed to take up, must be made in every case. Also reconnaissance of the flanks of the position held in case it may be necessary to form a defensive flank.

If a retirement is to take place of Cavalry when holding part of a line, this should not be carried out mounted. Led horses should first of all be got away and then the dismounted men should retire on foot. An instance of this occurred with HARMAN'S Force on the 26th March in the vicinity of DIVES. The French gave way on the left about CANDOR and Lieut.Col. COOK'S Detachment of the 2nd Cavalry Division had to withdraw. The withdrawal was carried out mounted with the result that confusion occurred and difficulty was experienced in taking up the appointed line in rear. Also, the fact of mounted men moving back has a demoralising effect on other troops, especially infantry, in the vicinity and is apt to cause premature withdrawals elsewhere. On the same day the withdrawal of the detachment of the 3rd Cavalry Division from BOIS D S ESSARTS was carried out by sending the horses away beforehand with satisfactory results.

5. Formation of defensive flanks requires more practice. Troops are too prone to retire and not to swing their flank, thereby causing neighbouring troops to retire. A defensive flank should be formed by a steady movement and swing round or advancing from the rear and not by a retrograde movement.

6. Led horses must be in charge of a senior Officer with others to help him. He should have a few spare mounted men as messengers and orderlies. The position of led horses must be changed frequently owing to shell fire and in some cases it was found difficult to keep touch with them.

......The importance

The importance of keeping led horses well opened out in small parties was emphasized when the 7th Dragoon Guards were ordered into reserve N.W. of VILLERS BRETONNEUX on the 4th April. Troops columns was found to be a suitable formation.

7. The type of trench which was constructed by units of this Division N.E. of VILLERS BRETONNEUX on the 4th April was a rifle pit about 4 feet 6" deep, 3 feet wide and anything up to 25 feet long. These trenches gave good protection against a heavy bombardment on the 5th April. Trenches were sited checkerwise according to ground.

II. MOUNTED ACTION.

On two occasions opportunities for mounted action occurred; (a) at VILLESELVE March 24th, (b) at the BOIS DE MOREUIL, March 30th.

The points brought out are:-

(a) The value of mounted action to restore a situation which has become critical. At VILLESELVE 100 prisoners were taken and a similar number of the enemy killed or wounded. The infantry, who were wavering, were able to advance again and re-establish themselves on their original line. The repulse of the enemy about VILLESELVE enabled the remnants of two Battalions of the 36th Division, who were cut off about CUGNY, to extricate themselves and the moral effect on our infantry of this local success was great.

(b) In the BOIS DE MOREUIL, the assistance rendered by the mounted attack on the enemy's flank and rear to the direct dismounted attack, which had been launched through the Wood from the N.W., is stated to have been considerable.

2. Mounted action-shock.

Infantry attack formation in waves worked well. Men should not be at too wide intervals, say 100 yards per troop; same distance between waves. Loud cheering to be encouraged. Rally sounded by trumpet.
This was exemplified at VILLESELVE.

3. Movement under fire.

6th Cavalry Brigade state that troop columns opened out worked well, but troop leaders still inclined to bunch.
7th Dragoon Guards, from experience gained E. of BOIS DE GENTELLES on 1st April, are of opinion that Squadrons in line in echelon present a much less vulnerable target than any kind of formation in half sections or depth.
It is generally agreed that the enemy is unable to make good shooting on a moving target such as a patrol.

4. Horse Management.

(6th Cav. Bde.)
With one man to 4 horses (and as was the case at one period, one man to 10 horses) it is almost impossible to look after horses for long periods properly. Saddlery and equipment are lost and watering and feeding is very difficult. Horses are kept saddled up unnecessarily long and suffer. More Officers and N.C.O's are required to be left behind.

.....In the

V. MACHINE GUNS.

6th M.G.
1. Machine gun fire should not be opened at long ranges except in organized attacks; the supply of ammunition is not sufficient for this and the harm done to the enemy is not great. Greater value is obtained by reserving the fire till the enemy are within effective range, i.e. 900 yards or less.

8th M.G.
2. Care must be taken to send all information possible to M.G. Commanders and the latter must ask for this. Any alterations in dispositions of the troops must be communicated to the Machine Guns. A case is quoted where, on April 4th, 2 sub-sections of M.G's went into action with a Regiment. That night the Regiment was withdrawn from the front line but the M.G. Officers were not told. One sub-section was thereby left in the line without orders and had to attach itself to some Infantry.

6th Cav. Bde.
On the other hand C.O's have brought forward that guns are moved about without their knowledge by the O.C. M.G. Squadron.

3. In some cases regimental officers gave orders to Machine Guns to deal with enemy Machine Guns. Such orders should, if possible, be given through a M.G. Officer as ammunition is sometimes scarce and he knows whether it can be spared. The targets were sometimes out of reasonable range.

4. As regards ammunition supply, the establishment of ammunition in belts was found insufficient. Runners coming back for more ammunition cannot afford to wait and fill belts from S.A.A. boxes. The question is being taken up separately.

8th M.G.
5. A Machine Gun Section has no Officer to send back with led horses, hence the Officer in charge of the led horses of the unit to which the Section is attached should be responsible for the led horses of the Section. In one case a subsection suffered severe casualties in horses owing to the N.C.O. i/c led horses not being told of the Regiment's withdrawal.

6. Both 6th and 8th M.G. Squadrons suggest that the pack saddles should be made wider in the arch, otherwise no complaints have been received regarding the equipment. The guns always fired well whatever the weather conditions. The belts in the latest pattern tin belt box always kept dry. Barr and Stroud range finders proved useful in the longer range fighting.

7. Indirect fire was little used, partly owing to lack of 1/20,000 maps but more because the opportunities for direct fire were so numerous.

VI. HOTCHKISS RIFLES.

1. Everyone speaks well of the Rifle when it is clean and properly handled. Dirt and mud are the great difficulties. Covers must be carried always.

When the position has been fixed, the Hotchkiss Rifles should be kept well under cover until required for firing. Cases occurred of Hotchkiss Rifles being put out by shell fire through being up on the parapet or above ground.

Officers report that Hotchkiss Rifles have a great moral effect on the enemy and are apparently difficult to locate. At

.....VILLERS BRETONNEUX

(7th D.G.)

In the case of led horses, the Officer in charge of the horses must be kept constantly informed of the tactical situation so that he can make arrangements for watering and feeding.

III. PATROLLING AND RECONNAISSANCE.

1. The work of patrols throughout the operations was excellent. In the case of HARMAN'S Force, the III Corps were quite in the dark as regards the situation until reconnaissances by Officer's patrols were carried out. It was the practice from March 23rd to 26th to keep 4 Officer's patrols - strength 1 Officer and 10 other ranks - at General HARMAN'S Headquarters, for employment as required. These patrols started out before dawn each day and were drawn in after dark. They worked in certain sectors of the front and supplied reliable information, not only of the position of the enemy's advancing troops, but also of our own infantry or of French troops. Reports were submitted every two hours, on an average, by mounted D.R. These patrol leaders were able to visit advanced Company, Regimental and Brigade Headquarters of Infantry or French units and send in a continuous stream of information of the situation on a front of 5 to 7 miles, which proved invaluable to the higher command. No casualties to patrols were reported although they worked often in front of our infantry in close touch with the enemy. The utmost self-reliance and bravery was shown.

In advancing to fill a gap which has occurred in the infantry line, patrols must be pushed well ahead to learn the situation and active patrolling is required to the flanks although other troops may be there. Stress cannot be laid too much on the necessity for very active reconnaissance taking place on moving in support of other units, in order to find out where those units actually are, and the dispositions and intentions of troops on either flank.

The above were exemplified during the operations of HARMAN'S Force and in the operation about VILLERS BRETONNEUX on 4/5th April. Owing to the somewhat shaken condition of the infantry, the flanks of the cavalry were often exposed without warning.

2. <u>Liaison with French Troops.</u>

It is the general opinion that liaison with French troops was bad. The average French Interpreter has no military knowledge or vocabulary and is quite useless for Liaison purposes. In the case of HARMAN'S Force, Liaison was carried out by means of French speaking British Officers; this was also done in the case of General SEELY's and General SEYMOUR's Forces (3rd Dismounted Division) which worked well.

IV. ARTILLERY.

Difficulty in communicating with our Artillery was experienced. This was due in many cases to the fact that the Cavalry were thrown in to fill a gap in the infantry line at short notice and some time elapsed before a proper liaison with the artillery covering that part of the front was established.

The general opinion is that in many cases positions could have been held and also great losses inflicted on the enemy infantry had it been possible to get into communication with the artillery quickly. In some cases losses were caused to our own men from our own artillery fire due to the artillery being ignorant of the exact situation of our troops.

........V.

2. The G.O.C. 6th Cavalry Brigade who was in command of the Dismounted Division attached to the 18th Division, reports that co-operation was unsatisfactory. Message containers though seen to fall from aeroplanes on two occasions could not be found - too small and inconspicuous.

Our M.Gs. were always in readiness to fire on hostile aeroplanes, but were not required except on one occasion when unfortunately M.Gs. were not there.

3. G.O.C. Canadian Cavalry Brigade reports that the capture of RIFLE WOOD was greatly facilitated by our low flying aeroplanes pouring M.G. fire into the enemy from a very low altitude.

IX. MEDICAL MATTERS.

1. The system adopted was to divisionalize the C.F.As. which worked under the A.D.M.S. Light Sections formed Advanced Dressing Stations and were echeloned, or placed where most convenient for the wounded. Heavy sections remained at a point in rear.

2. The evacuation of wounded in rearguard actions was difficult but few were abandoned. A shortage of stretchers was experienced, possibly due to a number having been lost with the Dismounted Division. The firing line was often considerably weakened by men employed in taking back wounded. Units complain that the C.F.A. do not send their stretcher bearers far enough forward, but on the other hand C.F.As. cannot spare, from their small establishment, men to go forward. It would seem that the best solution is for wounded to be kept in a covered place near the firing line till the situation is quieter and they can be removed. In rearguard actions officers naturally wish to get rid of casualties in case they have to retire and it has a bad moral effect on the men if they think they may be abandoned if wounded.

Motor or Horsed Ambulances should be pushed on far forward as possible with a view to relieving men carrying wounded.

3. A medical officer from the Field Ambulance should always be at Brigade Headquarters to control evacuation of wounded.

4. With the exception of the above points, Medical arrangements worked well.

X. TACTICS AND MORAL OF ENEMY.

The enemy's methods were to advance under cover of artillery and M.G. fire. If held in front he stopped, dug in and felt for a weak spot or an exposed flank and trickled through, thereby turning the position at which he had been checked.

His advance was often proceded by a smoke barrage.

His moral was good as long as he was having things his own way but when he saw he was up against determined men he shewed little inclination to come on.

VILLERS BRETONNEUX fire was opened at 2,000 yards which checked the enemy. It is considered, however, that fire should not be opened at long ranges but should be reserved until the enemy approaches within close range where the killing power is greater and the moral effect of surprise is obtained.

The Hotchkiss Rifle proved of great value in covering retirement in rearguard actions. Difficulty was experienced, however, in carrying rifles and strip boxes, etc., as the pack horses had been sent away, the result being that some equipment was lost. It is very necessary to have Hotchkiss pack horses when with the troops when a Dismounted Brigade is formed.

Two instances are given where the Hotchkiss Rifle proved its value:-

<u>17th L.</u>
(a) <u>March 26th.</u> A troop of 14 men and 1 Hotchkiss Rifle fought a rearguard action from HATTENCOURT to FOUQUESCOURT against greatly superior forces, enabling the infantry to get into position near the latter place and inflicting severe casualties on the enemy, the greater part of which were from Hotchkiss Rifle.

(b) <u>April 4th.</u> During enemy's attack towards VILLERS BRETONNEUX, a Hotchkiss Rifle did very great execution on masses of the enemy along the VILLERS BRETONNEUX main road, checking their attack. Range 800 yards.

VII. COMMUNICATIONS.

1. During the operations, the principal means of communication were:-

Corps to Divisional H.Q.	Telephone and D.R.
Divisional H.Q. to Brigades ...	D.R.(Motor cyclists and mounted men).
Brigades to Units	Mounted men mostly and motor cyclists where possible.

Visual was used on one or two occasions, notably between Divisional Headquarters at FOUILLOY and Brigade H.Q. on the 4th and 5th April. Lamp used.

2. Motor D.Rs. did excellent work throughout and there were very few cases of the miscarriage of orders.

3. The want of a Cable Section was keenly felt by the Divisional Signal Squadron.

4. Attached (Appendix B) is the report of the O.C. Divisional Signal Squadron, which embodies the points brought out during the operations.

VIII. AEROPLANES.

1. The Division being scattered in three different parties, there were no aeroplanes working directly with the Division, so little experience of co-operation with aeroplanes was gained.

........2.

Appendix "B" (continued)

COMMUNICATIONS.

VISUAL. Communication with the Brigades was established with Lucas. Whenever telephonic communication was cut this proved most valuable and several messages were sent and received.

TELEPHONE. Cable was laid forward to Brigades from Divisional H.Q. Owing to the fact that this had to be done by hand much time was wasted. Lines took a very long time to get through and were frequently cut by shell fire and troops. On the whole, communication was erratic and unreliable. This was due to the open country and lack of poles.

From FOUILLOY to BLANGY TRONVILLE open routes were used and these were also cut. Finally a Cable Wagon was borrowed from the 14th Division and cable laid forward.

MOUNTED DESPATCH RIDERS.

10 Mounted Despatch Riders were borrowed for Advanced Headquarters and they proved invaluable. Mounted men only could get from Advanced Divisional H.Q. to Brigades owing to the state of the ground and roads.

MOTOR CYCLISTS. The case in point shews that Motor Cyclists cannot be relied on to work forward of Advanced Divisional Headquarters. The weather was very bad, side roads were impracticable to Motor Cyclists and therefore Mounted D.R's took all messages.

WIRELESS. W/T set at FOUILLOY and /T at BLANGY TRONVILLE would have been very useful. On one occasion all routes, including Artillery, were cut forward, consequently the guns could not be got on to the targets at once.

ARTILLERY. Detached. It would have been impossible for this unit to have arranged communication for them. In consequence it is essential that a separate section should be allotted for Artillery Communication.

SUMMARY.

From the above it can be seen that the chief difficulty has been the insufficient means at hand for a Cavalry Divisional Signal Squadron to perform the duties now required of it. The chief difficulties are laying cable, Mounted D.Rs. and Visual Signallers. On the present establishment it is impossible to do all at once and very often the situation demands this being done.

On several occasions Visual Signallers were doing the work of a Cable Section and Mounted D.Rs., especially during the operations at VILLESELVE and PORQUERICOURT. This means that each form of communication is bound to suffer and the net result is a most elementary form of communication. If operations last for any considerable period the men soon get tired out with lack of sleep.

Cable wagons would have been invaluable during these cavalry operations, and at FOUILLOY a Cable Wagon had to be borrowed without which probably no communication would have been obtained forward to Advanced Headquarters. On the latter occasion it was of the utmost importance to lay cable forward to Brigades, to work a Visual Station and at the same time to keep up a supply of Mounted D.Rs. On the present establishment it is impossible to work all these at once. It is absolutely essential that these three means of communication should always be at hand. Three separate sections must be formed in a Signal Squadron to enable communications to be maintained properly, namely, a Visual Section, a Cable Section and a Mounted D.R. Section.

APPENDIX "B"

Report by O.C. 3rd Signal Squadron.

During the recent operations there have been two distinct phases :-

(a) General HARMAN'S Detachment, during which phase the Cavalry were acting chiefly as a mounted force.

(b) The operations at FOUILLOY, April 4/5th, when Cavalry were holding the line and the Division took over from the 14th Infantry Division.

(a) GENERAL HARMAN'S DETACHMENT.

DESPATCH RIDERS.

During these operations all communications forward rested entirely upon Mounted Despatch Riders and Motor Cyclists.
The visual signallers of this unit were used as Mounted Despatch Riders, thereby destroying any possibility of visual had it been possible.

TELEPHONE.

To the Corps, arrangements could generally be made through the nearest Infantry Division, but it always necessitated laying out cable by hand and this invariably took a certain amount of time when speed in laying out the line was most important.
Forward it was impossible to lay lines. On March 23/24 during the action at VILLESELVE cable might have been laid forward from BERLANCOURT to VILLESELVE which would have saved despatch riders. Owing to the length of time it takes to lay lines by hand, it was considered not worth while owing to the uncertainty of the situation.

VISUAL.

Was impracticable owing to the fact that the Visual Signallers were thought more valuable as Mounted Despatch Riders at the time.

WIRELESS.

No messages were sent by wireless during these operations.

AEROPLANES.

If contact patrol work could have been arranged it would have been most valuable, but arrangements were not made and consequently no messages were received from aeroplanes.

(b) THE FOUILLOY OPERATIONS.

GENERAL.

The Division moved forward as a Mobile Reserve to support the 14th Division. Advanced Headquarters were formed at FOUILLOY. After a short time the command of the sector was taken over by G.O.C. 3rd Cavalry Division. This included a Cavalry Detachment, 15th Australian Brigade and 43rd Infantry Brigade. The Signal Squadron had to arrange for communication with Cavalry acting as a mobile force and infantry holding the line. Later the situation resolved itself into Trench Warfare and 2 Offices were formed, one at FOUILLOY and the other at BLANGY TRONVILLE.

........COMMUNICATIONS.

Index..............

SUBJECT.

2

No.	Contents.	Date.
	General Harman	

NOT FOR
VISITORS

NARRATIVE OF OPERATIONS CARRIED OUT BY 3rd CAVALRY DIVISION
MARCH 21st to APRIL 5th 1918.

March 21st.
At 8 a.m. the 3rd Cavalry Division received orders from Cavalry Corps to be ready to move at 2 hours notice.

At 3:5 p.m. orders were received to move forthwith to an area about CUGNY coming under the orders of the III Corps. BEINE. Brigades got into bivouac about 10 p.m.

Dismounted Brigades were formed and the 6th Dismounted Brigade under Lieut Colonel Burt D.S.O. marched mounted to

March 22nd.
UGNY arriving there about 3 a.m. on the 22nd.

The Brigades proceeded thence by bus to OGNES where they came under the orders of the 58th Division.

The 7th Dismounted Brigade, Commanded by Lieut - Colonel E.Paterson, D.S.O. Iniskilling Dragoons, and the Canadian Dismounted Brigade, commanded by Lieut Colonel Macdonald, D.S.O M.C., both Brigades under the command of Brigadier General Seymour, D.S.O. marched mounted at 6 a.m. to VILLEQUIER-AUMONT and thence on foot to FRIERES Camp, about 1 mile N.E. of VILLEQUIER AUMONT.

The led horses of these Brigades and remainder of the Division marched to an area VARESNES, BRETIGNY, PONTOISE.

The operations of General Seymour's force (7th and Canadian Dismounted Brigades) from 22nd - 25th are given in Appendix I, and those of 6th Dismounted Brigade in Appendix II.

March 23rd.
At 9:50 a.m. March 23rd the Division was notified by telephone that the Germans had broken through the line at HAM, and was ordered to turn out as many mounted men as possible.

Orders were issued to Brigades to turn out 50 mounted men per regiment, the Column to concentrate as soon as possible, under Lieut-Colonel Paterson, Canadian Brigade, at the cross-roads, BRETIGNY, and thence to proceed via GRANDRU to BUCHOIRE, III Corps H.Q.

On reporting to III Corps H.Q. General Harman was ordered to take command of the mounted detachments of 2nd and 3rd Cavalry Divisions, also Colonel Theibald's Infantry, 600 strong, a Detachment of No. 13 Balloon Company, consisting of 8 Lewis Guns and personnel, one lorry and one tender, and "O" Battery R.H.A. The whole force was to be known as Harman's Detachment with Headquarters at BERLANCOURT.

By 1 p.m. Harman's Detachment (less Theobald's Infantry and "O" Battery) was concentrated in position of readiness at BERLANCOURT and Officers' patrols were sent out as follows:-

BEAUMONT, to get touch with General Greenly.
BROUCHY-BAUCOURT-OLLEZY, to get touch with enemy.
BERLANCOURT-MUILLE VILETTE-HAM, to get touch with enemy.
ESMERY HALLON-CANIZY, to get touch with enemy.

Strength of Harman's Detachment was now approximately as follows:-

2nd Cav. Div. Mounted Detachment C.O. Capt. Bonham.	300
3rd Cav. Div. Mounted Detachment C.O. Lt.COL. Paterson, D.S.O.	450
	750 Mounted men
Theobald's Detachment C.O. Lt. Col Theobald.	600 Infantry
Detachment No.13 Balloon Company with 8 Lewis Guns.	38

"O" Battery R.H.A.

Light Section, 7th Cavalry Field Ambulance.

Theobald's Infantry and "O" Battery R.H.A. joined at BERLANCOURT about 4:30 p.m. and shortly afterwards III Corps placed Harman's Detachment at the disposal of General Greenly. Commanding 14th Division.

At 6:45 p.m., orders were received from 14th Division to fill up a gap on the left of their support line from cross-roads 1000 yards E of VILLESELVE Church to Hill 81. This order was cancelled 15 minutes later by a galloper from 14th Division, and 2nd and 3rd Cavalry Division Detachments were ordered instead to fill up a gap on the right of 14th Division line between VILLEQUIR AUMONT and LA NEUVILLE-EN-BEINE.

On proceeding to UGNY for this purpose, it was found that General Seymour was already occupying this line with his dismounted force. Lt. COL. Paterson telephoned to G.O.C. 14th Division and received instructions to bivouac the night at UGNY and return to BERLANCOURT early the next morning.

At 11 p.m. orders were received to send Theobald's Infantry to block the Western exits of VILLESELVE which was done, Col Theobald and No. 13 Balloon Company taking up a position in a semi-circle on the Western side of, and about 300 yards from, VILLESELVE. "O" Batty was sent to a position N.E. of BERLANCOURT to cover VILLESELVE.

During the day, Divisional H.Q. Rear, all led horses and "B" Echelon moved to the CARLSPONT area under the command of Brigadier General Portal, D.S.O.

March 24th.

At 7:30 a.m. March 24th 14th Division issued orders that 2nd and 3rd Cavalry Division Detachments of Harman's Detachment were to be employed in protecting the left flank of 14th Division by filling a gap in the line from cross-roads 1000 yards E. of VILLESELVE Church to Hill 81. Theobald's Infantry was to remain in position of VILLESELVE.

3rd Cavalry Division Detachment was sent to carry out this task with "O" Battery in position to support them.

2nd Cavalry Division Detachment was kept in reserve at BERLANCOURT.

At 11:10 a.m. a telephone message was received from III Corps ordering Harman's Detachment to clear up the situation between ESMERY HALLEN and GOLANCOURT. 2nd Cavalry Division Detachment was sent forward for this purpose.

At 11:50 a.m. a message was received from 14th Division notifying their withdrawal through 9th French Division and ordering Harman's Detachment to continue to protect the left flank of 9th French Division.

A Staff Officer reported to 9th French Division H.Q.

1:30 p.m. and received verbal orders to move the whole of Harman's Detachment as rapidly as possible to BEAUGIES and take up a position between BEAUGIES and CREPIGNY to protect 9th French Division right flank.

This order could not be carried out because 2nd Cavalry Division Detachment was in action near ESMERY HALLON and 3rd Cavalry Division Detachment near VILLESELVE, and it was impossible to withdraw either force.

9th French Division were notified and said that as they could not have the cavalry they did not want Theobald's Detachment which by now numbered about 400 only.

The order which had been sent to Theobald's Detachment to concentrate at BERLANCOURT on first receipt of 9th French Division order was therefore cancelled, and they remained in position W. of VILLESELVE.

About 2:30 p.m. 3rd Cavalry Division Detachment came into action mounted N. of VILLESELVE. As a result of this action 100 prisoners were taken, about 100 enemy sabred, and the remains of 2 Battalions which were surrounded at CUGNY were enabled to extricate themselves. A full account of this action is given in Appendix III.

At 4:55 p.m. orders were issued to Units of Harman's Detachment to withdraw to GUISCHARD, mounted troops covering the retirement of all Infantry in the vicinity until GUISCHARD was reached, and then to come into reserve at MUIRANCOURT.

Headquarters of the Detachment moved to MUIRANCOURT.

These orders were duly carried out, except that 2nd Cavalry Detachment remained in neighbourhood of FRENICHES.

Under orders of III Corps, Lieut Col Reynolds, Commanding Northumberland Hussars, drew 120 horses from the 24/25th and with the 120 men of his regiment thus mounted joined General Harman's Force at 8 a.m.

March 25th

Divisional H.Q. Rear with "B" Echelon and led horses moved to OLLENCOURT before noon. 650 led horses per Brigade were left at CARLEPONT for the dismounted Brigades of General Seymour's and Co. Burt's Forces. The 7th and Canadian Brigades took over those horses during the afternoon. Owing to the tactical situation it was impossible to withdraw the 6th Dismounted Brigade from the line on the 25th.

At 1:50 a.m. March 25th, enemy were reported in close proximity to GUISCHARD, and at 3:20 a.m. under orders issued by III Corps to General Harman' personally, the Detachment less Theobald's Infantry concentrated at LAGNY. Colonel Theobald's Infantry was ordered to move to BEAURAINS and come under the orders of the Brigadier General there.

At 9:15 a.m. Colonel Cook's Detachment of 2nd Cavalry Division, 500 strong, was placed unde the orders of General Harman. They were, however, operating in the vicinity of BEAURAINS under 14th Division.

At 1:30 p.m. orders were received from the 14th Division to the effect that Harman's Detachment would act under the orders of 10th French Division.

G.O.C. 10th French Division ordered Harman's Detachment to act in co-operation with French Infantry Regimental Commander at CATIGNY. As a result of an interview with this Officer, the following dismounted party was ordered up to a reserve position immediately S.W. of MUIRANCOURT at 3 p.m.

O.C. Col. Paterson, D.S.O.

3rd Cavalry Division Party	350 men
2nd " " "	250 "
	600

Col Cook's Detachment concentrated at LAGNY for this purpose and Col. Cook assumed command of 2nd Cavalry Division Detachment. At 6 p.m. Col. Paterson reported the French to be retiring from MUIRANCOURT; he was consequently ordered to retire to his horses, mount and protect the retirement of the French Infantry.

This he did and then took up a line between the River and the main road from CATIGNY - SERMAIZE.

March 26th.

About 4 a.m. Brigadier General Portal received orders by telephone from Lieut-General Butler, Commanding III Corps, to collect a force of all available mounted men from CARLEPONT, OLLENCOURT and BAILLY (2nd Cav. Division Details), and assemble as a Corps Reserve at LES CLOYES (P 20). Strong patrols were to be sent to SEMPIGNY and PONTOISE and the enemy was to be prevented from crossing the river OISE. Communication was to be established with 18th Division at CAISNES and with General Pitman, commanding Mounted Detachment of 2nd Cavalry Division at CHIRY. In compliance with these orders a force consisting of 650 mounted men, together with 3rd Field Squadron R.E. was concentrated at LES CLOYES at 7:30 a.m. on the morning of 27th. The 7th and Canadian Brigades Detachments from CARLEPONT joined the force at 9:30 a.m. The narrative of the operations of this force is given in Appendix IV.

The remainder of Divisional H.Q. Rear with led horses and "B" Echelon divisionalized marched to CHOISY AU BAC just N. of COMPIEGNE. Brigades bivouacked along the N edge of the FORET DE COMPIEGNE with "B" Echelons and Reserve Park in the forest. Divisional H.Q. Rear was established in CHOISY with General Seylour in command.

At 3:30 a.m. March 26th, Harman's Detachment withdrew through the French Infantry to reserve at DIVES, remaining under the orders of G.O.C. 10th French Division.

At 9:50 a.m. enemy were reported to have entered the BOIS DES ESSARTS. 2nd Cavalry Division Detachment were consequently ordered to move to the Fme. CHARBONNEAUX (Square I.1.b.) and take up a position running N.W. and S.E. through that place. 3rd Cavalry Division Detachment to BOIS DES CUBISTES in support and "O" Battery to North of BOIS DE LA RESERVE.

At 10:35 a.m 3rd Cavalry Division Detachment was ordered to attack and occupy high ground in BOIS DES ESSARTS about I.9.central. Details of this action/are given in Appendix V.

Harman's Detachment then withdrew to THIESCOURT, reformed and then went into Reserve at ELINCOURT.

March 27th.
At 9 a.m. orders were received from III Corps for all details of 2nd Cavalry Division and Canadian Cavalry Brigade to move forthwith to VENETTE (W. of COMPIEGNE) were they would come under the orders of G.O.C. 2nd Cavalry Division.

The remainder of Harman's Detachment was placed under the orders of Lieut Col. Reynolds (12th Lancers), Commanding Northumberland Hussars. This Detachment, to be known as Reynold's Force, was composed as follows:-

	Officers.	O.R.
6th Cavalry Brigade Detachment	5	89
7th " " "	4	125
Northumberland Hussars.	6	70
	15	284

together with 2 Vickers Guns from a M.M.G. Battery.

It was placed under the orders of General Perkins, Commanding III Corps H.A. for reconnaissance work and was billeted at CHEVINCOURT.

"O" Battery was placed under the orders of 14th D.A.

During 27th night 27/28th, 28th and night 28/29th this force was employed patrolling the line CHIRY - THIESCOURT - BASSIGNY - CANNY - BIERMONT.

This front was now held entirely by French Troops supported by British Artillery. The information obtained by the patrols as to the position of the French and enemy forces was of great value to the British Artillery.

General Harman with his staff rejoined the Division at CHOISY on the morning of the 27th. General Portal's Force less 1 Squadron of the Inniskilling Dragoons, arrived at CHOISY during the afternoon. Col. Burt's Force (6th Dismounted Brigade) also rejoined.

The Division was therefore reconstituted with the following exceptions :-
(a) Canadian Cav. Bde. attached 2nd Cavalry Division.
(b) About 200 men of 6th and 7th Brigades with Reynold's Fce.
(c) 1 Squadron Inniskilling Dragoons remaining in observation about LES CLOYES.

<u>March 28th.</u> Division remained at CHOISY.

<u>March 29th.</u> The Division marched North towards AMIENS, Divisional H.Q. for the night being situated at LES MESNIL-SUR-BULLES, (5 miles E. of St. JUST - EN - CHAUSSEE).

The detachments of the 3rd Cavalry Division from Reynolds Force and the Squadron Inniskilling Dragoons rejoined the Division. "O" Battery remained with 14th D.A.

<u>March 30th.</u> The Division marched to SAINS-EN-AMIENOIS, "Q" Rear with "A"2 and "B" Echelons to WAILLY.

<u>March 31st.</u> 3rd Cavalry Division (less Canadian Cavalry Brigade) situated in SAINS-EN-AMIENOIS Area.

3 p.m. received Fifth Army No.G.292 ordering Division to be prepared to move at short notice and placing 3rd Cavalry Division under orders of XIX Corps.

7:30 p.m. XIX Corps order No.G.316 received, ordering 3rd Cavalry Division to concentrate in vicinity of BOIS DE GENTELLES by 8 a.m. April 1st.

<u>April 1st.</u> This concentration was complete by 7:30 a.m. April 1st and Divisional Headquarters established at North end of BOVES.

10:50 a.m. Orders received to place one Brigade at disposal of G.O.C. 2nd Cavalry Division for use if required to retain ground gained that morning. 7th Brigade detailed. G.O.C. 7th Cavalry Brigade was already in touch with G.O.C. 2nd Cavalry Division.

The Inniskillings moved forward at 11 a.m. to HOURGES;

the 7th Dragoon Guards at 1:30 p.m. to BOMART sur la LUCE. Both regiments came under orders of G.O.C. Canadian Cavalry Brigade (who was under orders of 2nd Cavalry Division) and were employed repelling counter-attack against RIFLE WOOD (C.10. and 11.) and holding the wood that night.

4:40 p.m. Received orders from XIX Corps for 3rd Cavalry Division, including troops detached, to concentrate that evening in Wood E.34.c. 2 miles N.W. of GLETELIES. 6th Cavalry Brigade and 3rd Field Squadron moved forwith. 7th Cavalry Brigade completed their move, after having been relieved, at 6:45 a.m. April 2nd.

April 2nd.

8:30 a.m. 3rd Field Squadron was placed at disposal of G.O.C. 18th Division for work on the CACHY Switch Line.

9:30 a.m. State of readiness - Off Saddled but prepared to move off at half an hours notice.

10:20 a.m. XIX Corps notified 3rd Cavalry Division that one Brigade might be placed at disposal of G.O.C. 1st Cavalry Division that night.

11:00 a.m. Canadian Brigade having come under orders of 3rd Cavalry Division was ordered to concentrate in the BOIS DE BOVES.

An account of the operations of the Canadian Brigade from March 29th to April 1st is given in Appendix VI.

2. p.m. 3rd Cavalry Division Report centre moved to BLANGY TRONVILLE.

5:25 p.m. Orders from XIX Corps to place one Brigade at disposal of G.O.C. 1st Cavalry Division, 6th Cavalry Brigade detailed and employed as follows:-

April 3rd.

One Regiment digging posts during night of 2nd/3rd in the "P" Line. On completion of work Regiment bivouacked about 10.27.

One Regiment moved to vicinity of BOUILLOY at 6 a.m.
3rd, to be in mobile reserve/ready to move at half an hours notice.

Infantry of 14th Division.   P.8.central to VAIRE-SOUS-CORBIE.

17th Lancers in support of 3rd Dragoon Guards and Royals

7th Dragoon Guards about to be sent to reinforce 10th Hussars.

About 2 p.m. Lieut. Col. Burt, Commanding 3rd Dragoon Guards and Royals reported that he had the situation well in hand.

At 4:30 p.m. Brigadier General A.L.P.Harman, D.S.O. Commanding 3rd Cavalry Division, received orders by telephone from XIX Corps to take over command of the left Sector from Major General Skinner, Commanding 14th Division.

At 5 p.m. 15th Australian Brigade was placed at the disposal of G.O.C. 3rd Cavalry Division. Two Battalions of the Brigade had already been moved to reinforce the left of the 14th Division about VAIR - SOUS - CORBIE.

At 8 p.m. 15th Australian Brigade was ordered to take over the line from the WARFUSSEE ABANCOURT - FOUILLOY road to the SOMME, relieving units of the 14th Division, the 10th Hussras and the 7th Dragoon Guards then in that line, and the 6th Cavalry Brigade to take over the line from St. QUENTIN - AMIENS road (inclusive) at P.25.c.8.2. to the WARFUSSEE ABANCOURT - FOUILLOY road (exclusive) at P.20.a.0.9.

This relief was completed at 5 a.m. April 5th and all units of the 7th Cavalry Brigade placed under the orders of G.O.C. 6th Cavalry Brigade.

The 43rd Infantry Brigade on relief remained in reserve under orders of G.O.C. 3rd Cavalry Division concentrated about P.24.a.

The 11th Kings, under orders of G.O.C. 43rd Infantry Brigade, were ordered to dig and occupy a line of posts from about O.30. central - O.24.d. central - O.18.d. central All M.G's remained in the line. They consisted of the Following :-

M.G.'s of 1st Cavalry Division.

M.G&s of 3rd. Cavalry Division.

16th Machine Gun Battalion.

14th   "   "   "

16th Divisional Artillery continued to cover from taken over by 3rd Cavalry Division.

Led horses of 3rd Cavalry Division were moved back to N.34.c.

The Canadian Cavalry Brigade in the BOIS DE BOVES had been ordered to off-saddle at 5:10 p.m.

The night of 4/5th was uneventful.

April 5th.   At 11 a.m. on the 5th, the enemy attacked on the whole Divisional Front after an intense bombardment of 45 minutes duration.

6th Cavalry Brigade and 15th Australian Infantry Brigade reported attack was stopped by M.G. and Artillery Fire.

15th Australian Infantry reported repulse of attack by telephone.

6th Cavalry Brigade report as follows:-
"G.B.156."   5th   Timed 1:10 p.m.
Lt. Col. Burt reports that the whole of his front has been bombarded heavily. His casualties are very small AAA Strong attack developed on his whole front about 11 a.m. This attack was stopped dead by M.G. and Arty. AAA Enemy forming up again about 12:45 p.m. AAA Col Burt reports he is strongly dug in and is confident of being able to deal with the situation AAA 7th Cavalry Brigade equally happy AAA Ends.

The Artillery were informed of massing of enemy referred to in 6th Cavalry Brigade report. No attack developed.

At 3 p.m. 5th Australian Division was ordered to relieve 3rd Cavalry Division in Left sector.

The relief was completed uneventfully at 4 a.m. April 6th and 3rd Cavalry Division moved to C MON area on the 6th and came into III Corps reserve, and subsequently rejoined Cavalry Corps.

APPENDIX 1

Narative of Operations of 3rd Dismounted Division.
March 22nd - 25th 1918.

March. 22nd.

Headquarters, 6th Cavalry Brigade formed Headquarters 3rd Dismounted Division at 7 a.m. 22nd March and established their headquarters at VILLEQUIER AUMONT.

6th Dismounted Brigade moved by bus at 1 a.l. to OGNES, on arrival there to come under the orders of 58th Division.

7th and Canadian Dismounted Brigades were encamped in the Wood in huts at S.14. central FRIERES Wood, by 10 a.m. with 8th and 9th Canadian Machine Gun Squadrons, 8 and 12 machine guns respectively.

The 3rd Dismounted Division were in III Corps reserve.

Owing to uncertainty of situation about TERGNIER, 7th Dismounted Brigade were placed under orders of 18th Divn. and 35 busses were sent to be ready to move them about 2:30 p.m. but 7th Dismounted Brigade only "Stood to" at ½ hours notice.

H.Q. and Canadian Dismounted Brigade were to remain in III Corps Reserve.

2:30 p.m. Message received from G.O.C. III Corps that it was his intention to prevent the enemy crossing the CROZAT Canal; and that in consequence various adjustments between the 14th, 18th and 58th Divisional Sectors would take place. The 3rd, 4th and 5th Cavalry Dismounted Brigades were put at the disposal of the 14th Division, 6th Dismounted Brigade was to remain at the disposal of 58th Division. The 7th Cavalry Dismounted Brigade was to be at the disposal of the 18th Division and the Canadian Cavalry Dismounted, Brigade to remain in Corps reserve in FRIERES WOOD.

3:5 p.m. 7th Dismounted Brigade ordered to prepare to enbuss under order of the 18th Division. 35 busses arrived General Lee (G.O.C. 18th Division) and G.O.C. 3rd Dismounted Division went to FRIERES WOOD, where they sited 6 Machine Guns of 7th Dismounted Brigade.

3:45 p.m. Canadian Dismounted Brigade placed at the disposal of 18th Division and ordered to send Officers to reconnoitre routes to VOUEL (T.19.c.)

8:15 p.m. 7th Dismounted Brigade ordered to occupy defences on the Eastern Edge of FRIERES WOOD from the PHEASANTRY Southwards for about 1000 Yards.

9:55 p.m. 18th Division ordered half of Canadian Dismounted Brigade to be placed at the disposal of General Sadleir Jackson (G.O.C. 54th Infantry Brigade) as a Reserve (not to be used in counter-attack). One section of Machine Gun Squadron to accompany.

11 p.m. 7th Dismounted Brigade in position as ordered with 7th Dragoon Guards on the right and in touch with the Queens, 17th Lancers of the left, and in touch with East Surreys, and Inniskilling Dragoons in reserve on main road S.15.b.9.0.

March 23rd.   2:45 a.m. Canadian Dismounted Brigade report 4 machine guns being sent to 54th Brigade.

9:0 a.m. One Regiment Canadian Dismounted Brigade moved to 54 Brigade.

9:30 a.m. Whole of the Canadian Dismounted Brigade under orders of 18th Division, were placed at the disposal of 54th Brigade.

11:30 a.m. Two Squadron, Inniskilling Dragoons sent to reinforce the 7th Dragoon Guards.

12:15 p.m. 7th Dismounted Brigade report that troops on their right were gradually retiring, both French and British, and they were being forced to prolong their right to conform. The 3rd Squadron Inniskilling Dragoons was consequently sent to the right to form a defensive flank.

12:30 pm. 7th Dismounted Brigade placed at disposal of G.O.C. 55th Brigade.

1 p.m. Under order of 18th Division, the 3rd Dismounted Division moved to UNGY. The 6th Cavalry Field Ambulance remained at VILLEQUIR AUMONT, sending one

Medical Officer and one Ambulance each to the 7th and Canadian Dismounted Brigades.

6 p.m. Owing to news being received that the Germans were getting round VILLEQUIER AUMONT from N.W. and were approaching UGNY from the woods to the North, the G.O.C. 3rd Dismounted Division was ordered by G.O.C.18th Division to assume command of details in UGNY, and to take up a position on the high ground to the N.E. of the village overlooking GUYENCOURT.

By 8:30 a.m. about 2000 men consisting of YPF men 2nd Cavalry Division, Entrenching Battalion and Infantry Details, with Machine Guns, were in position, and began to dig themselves in. The 7th Dismounted Brigade, having been relieved by the French, here joined the Division. At 9:30 p.m. the 1st French Dismounted Cavalry Division and the 9th French Infantry Division had passed through and taken up a position near VILLEQUIER AUMONT. The force under General Seymour then withdrew.

The Canadian Dismounted Brigade rejoined about 10 p.m. and bivouacked in the BOIS CAUMONT.

March 24th.   Infantry details were handed over to AFM 18th Division at CAILLOUEL, for despatch to their units.

The 3rd Dismounted Division with about 600 other ranks of the 2nd Dismounted Division marched to CAILLOUEL, where they camped for three hours. Owing to the ~~continuation~~ continuance of the German advance, the 18th Division wished to clear the village to facilitate the passage of heavy artillery. The 3rd Dismounted Division and 2nd Cavalry details consequently marched to bivouac immediately West of DAMPCOURT.

4 p.m. General Seeley assumed command of 2nd and 3rd Dismounted Divisions, with Headquarters at APPILLY, and at the same time the Dismounted Cavalry came under the orders of General Dibold, Commanding 125th French Infantry Divn.

DAMPCOURT and the bivouac were shelled between 6 and 7pm

Posts were put out between the OISE Canal and the NOYON-CHAUNY Road.

March 25th.
4 a.m. The 2nd Cavalry Division details were withdrawn to their horses and went to VARESNES, where they rejoined their own Division.

4:15 a.m. Owing to the enemy forcing back the French The 3rd Dismounted Division was ordered to take up a defensive position round APPILLY to cover their retirement

9:0 a.m. The following were the dispositions:-
1 Squadron Lord Strathcona's Horse was in MONDESCOURT. The 17th Lancers and Inniskilling Dragoons held a line from the X Road NOYON - CHAUNY - CREPIGNY - DAMPCOURT to the Canal, with the 7th Dragoon Guards thrown back to form a defensive flank to the South. The Royal-Canadian Dragoons were at PETIT QUIERCY where they had been sent to help Colonel Pichat, and 5 Squadrons were in reserve at the chateau at APPILLY.

11:0 a.m. under orders of the III Corps, all the Cavalry were withdrawn from the line, concentrated at BRETIGNY, and marched back independently to their horses at CARLEPONT. The enemy occupied APPILLY about 1:30 p.m. crossed the canal and took up a position north of the OISE, the French holding the line of the river.

Narrative and Diary of Operations of 3rd Cavalry Division from August 6th to August 11th 1918.

Reference 1/40,000 - Sheets 62D & 62E.

NARRATIVE.

Date.	Time.	
Aug. 6th.		4th Bde. R.H.A. & R.C.H.A. Bde. moved from BEAUCOURT (Daily Mail Woods) to Area N. & S.W. of AMIENS - Batteries to Brigade Areas as under. 3rd Cavalry Division Order No.38.
	9 a.m.	3rd Cavalry Division order No.40 issued.
	9:11 p.m.	Q.F. Wagons from D.A.C. two Batteries in Brigades Areas.
Night 6th/7th		Division moved from YZEUX - BOURDON - SOUES Area to bivouacs W. & S.W. of AMIENS as follows:-
		6th Cavalry Brigade to HENENCOURT.
		7th Cavalry Brigade to MONTIERES.
		Canadian " to AMIENS. Public Gardens.
		Divisional Troops. to PONT -DE- METZ.
		" H'q YZEUX to PONT -DE- METZ.
		(3rd Cavalry Division Order No. 39.)
		Concentration as above completed by 4 a.m. 7th
7th	a.m.	"B" Echelons, Heavy Sec. C.F.As, Heavy Sect. Res:Park concentrated in SOUES Area (3rd Cavalry Division Order No. 39).
		Dismounted party and reserve of Instructors to ABBE-VILLE by train from HANGEST.
	4 p.m.	3 M.V.S. divisionalized at PONT-DE-METZ.
Night 7th/8th		Division moved to Assembly Area 2 miles East of LONGUEAU.)

NARRATIVE

Date	Time	
Night 7th/8th		Divisional Hd. Qrs. PONT-DE-METZ to TRONVILLE WOOD (S. end) } 3rd Cavalry Division Order
		A.T. & A.T. Echelons divisionalized. } No. 41.
		A.H.T. attached to D.A.C. for operations. } q
8th.	2:30 a.m.	Concentration of fighting troops and A.T. Echelon in assembly Area completed.
		One Squadron L.S. Horse advanced to about CACHY with patrols in touch with Infantry.
		Special patrols ready to reconnoitre crossings over River LUCE.
	4.20 a.m.	Zero Hour - Canadian Corps attacked from AMIENS - ROYE road to AMIENS - CHAULNES railway. 5 mile front
	5.40 a.m.	Division moved forward to CACHY - Canadian Brigade leading, followed by 7th Cavalry Brigade and 6th Cavalry Brigade. Advanced Divl. H.Q. to CACHY U.2.b. (62.D.)
	7:25 a.m.	Remainder L.S. Horse "B" Battery R.C.H.A. & 4 M.Gns ordered forward to vicinity of MORGEMONTWOOD to ascertain position of Infantry of 1st and 3rd Canadian Infantry Divisions.
	7.45 a.m.	Remainder of Canadian Cavalry Brigade to MORGEMONT WOOD with 2 Companies of Tanks (whippets).
8th	8 a.m.	MORGEMONT WOOD reported still held by M.G., Tanks engaging.
	8:30 a.m.	MORGEMONT WOOD reported clear of enemy and Infantry pushing on.
	8:55 a.m.	Adv. Divl. H.Q. CACHY to pt. 2m E of MORGEMONT WOOD.
	9:15 a.m.	7th Cavalry Brigade ordered up behind Canadian Cavalry Brigade.
	9:15 a.m.	Adv. Divl. H.Q. 2m East of MORGEMONT WOOD.
	9:15 a.m.	Patrol from Fort Garry Horse reported two crossings at IGNAUCOURT fit for Cavalry and one fit for tanks.
	9:20 a.m.	Canadian Cavalry Brigade commenced crossing River LUCE at IGNAUCOURT, with one Squadron L.S. Horse as

NARRATIVE.

Date	Time.	
		advance guard - 45 prisoners and 1 gun captured.
	9:55 a.m.	7th Cavalry Brigade ordered to cross LUCE at IGNAUCOURT behind Canadian Cavalry Brigade.
	10.25 a.m.	Canadian Cavalry Brigade concentrated S. of R. LUCE about IGNAUCOURT and 1 Regiment with 8 Whippet Tanks moved west of wood in D.10.c. to the AMIENS - ROYE road.
	10.30 to 11.0 a.m.	1 Regiment (L.S. Horse) Canadian Cavalry Brigade reached ROYE Road and gained touch with Independent Force (C.M.M.G. Bde) about MAISON BLANCHE.
	10:55 a.m.	L.S.H. swung left handed between MEZIERES and BEAUCOURT - EN - SANTERRE to Valley in D.28.B.Sq. capturing 40 prisoners.
		Two troops were directed on FRESNOY-EN-CHAUSSEE where 125 prisoners were captured.
		R.C.D. with 8 tanks moved to N. of BEAUCOURT. Remainder of Canadian Cavalry Brigade to a position about D.16.d.5.0.
	11 a.m.	Adv. Divl. H.Q. moved from E. of MORGEMONT WOOD (V.13.c) via DEMUIN crossing to about D.9.d. followed by 6th Cavalry Brigade.
	11.10 a.m.	7th Cavalry Brigade moved forward from point of concentration S. of R. LUCE as follows:-
		One Regt. (Inniskilling) thro' D.10. and D.17. to capture Woods E. of BEAUCOURT and in touch with Canadian Cavalry Brigade on their right.
		One Regt. (7th D.G.) round N. edge of Copse in D.ll.a. capturing a few prisoners and 5 M.G's in copse at D.ll.d. which was attacked by one Sqdn. 7th D.Gds.

Date	Time.	NARRATIVE.

One Sqdn 7th D.Gds. capturing enemy position through D.18. central to S. edge of CAYEUX WOOD -
Casualties heavy - 100 prisoners and 5 M.G's taken.
Remainder Sqdn 7th D.G's attack on S. edge of CAYEUX WOOD taking a few prisoners and 6 heavy guns.
One Regt. (17th Lancers) were launched against N. edge of CAYEUX WOOD via valley in D.5.d.
This completed first bound of 7th Cavalry Brigade.

11:20 a.m. to 12:0 p.m. — Inniskillings on right of 7th Cavalry Brigade held up at D.17.c. by M.G. fire from Wood E. of BEAUCOURT. Later a counter-attack was beaten off. Several prisoners and one anti-tank gun captured.

11:40 a.m. — Adv. Divl. H.Q. established at D.9.b.

8th Cavalry Brigade concentrated in support behind Divl. H.Q. about D.3.c. & d.

8th 11:10 a.m. — Canadian Cavalry Brigade met strong resistance on line J.6.central-D.24.d. from enemy in a line of pits. Tanks were sent against this position but forced by heavy gun fire to retire.

12:0 — A line was then taken up and held as follows:- D.28.a.&.b.-D.23.central-D.23.b.5.9.
Detachments sent into J.5.a.&.b. rounded up and brought in 70 prisoners and captured many M.G8s.

12:30 p.m. — SITUATION. Canadian Cavalry Brigade on first objective on line mentioned above E. of BEAUCOURT and in touch with 7th Cavalry Brigade about D.17.c. Line continued by 7th Cavalry Brigade D.18.a.-D.12.d.-D.7.a.
Canadian Cavalry Brigade in touch with Independent force at D.28.a.

1 p.m. — One Regt. (Royals) from 6th Cavalry Brigade sent to reinforce 7th Cavalry Brigade.

1:40 p.m. — Following orders received/issued.-
6th Cavalry Brigade. (less 1 Regt) to right flank of 7th Cavalry Brigade with instructions to turn

Date.	Time.	NARRATIVE.
		BEAUCOURT WOODS from N. and N.E. and the to push on and seize objectives originally alloted to Canadian Cavalry Brigade on "Blue dotted" line E. of LE QUESNEL. 7th Cavalry Brigade, with Royals to push on to Blue dotted line and occupy final objectives E.22.a.- E.27 central. Canadian Cavalry Brigade. to reorganise and concentrate in support about D.17.b. and D.18.a. so soon as line gained by them E. of BEAUCOURT had been taken over by Canadian Infantry.
	2:30p.m.	Final objective E.16.c.7.0. to E.26.d.9.5. occupied by 7th Cavalry Brigade with one Regt. (17th Lancers)- 38 prisoners, 3 M.G. 3 Field Hospitals and several Guns captured.
	3 p.m.	Royals ordered by O.C. 7th Cavalry Brigade to push on beyond final objective to line WARVILLERS- VRELY. Instructions received from Cavalry Corps (G.10) that in event of high ground E.16.-E.22. being occupied by 7th Cavalry Brigade, 2nd Cavalry Division will push on through them in direction of ROYE, leaving 3rd Cavalry Division to occupy line of outer AMIENS defences (Blue dotted line)
	3:15 p.m.	6th Cavalry Brigade (less Royals) moved toCaulley E.9.c. 7th Cavalry Brigade to E.21.a. One Regt. ordered to push onto BEAUFORT-LE QUESNEL Road and a Sqdn. seized a position at head of valley E.27.d. Remainder of Regt. unable to advance owing to heavy M.G. fire from direction of BEAUFORT and the spur N.E. of LE QUESNEL. E.3.a. & c.
	4:10 p.m.	One Regt. (royals) 6th Cavalry Brigade occupying posts from E.15.b.9.0. to E.21.b.9.0. with one Sqdn. holding Southern edge of wood E.15. Held up by M.G. fire from BEAUFORT.

NARRATIVE.

Date	Time.	
8th	4:45 to 5:45 p.m.	10th Hussars ordered to send patrols forward and advance round left flank of Royals through E.22.b. & E.23.c.- This was unsuccessful.
	4.30 p.m.	12th Canadian Infantry Brigade arrived and took over line held by 7th Cavalry Brigade. Adv. Div. H.Q. at D.18.d.6.3. (BEAUCOURT-CAIX Road). Canadian Cavalry Brigade concentrated in support about D.17.b. & 18.a.- Infantry having taken over their line E. of BEAUCOURT.
	5.30 p.m.	Orders issued for 6th and 7th Cavalry Brigades to remain on line now held.
	6:0p.m. to 7 p.m.	Situation. Left of 6th Cavalry Brigade held by one Regt. from E.15.b.9.0. to S. edge of wood E.21.b. in touch with 1st Cavalry Division - Line also held by 12th Canadian Infantry Brigade. Right of 6th Cavalry Brigade held by one Regt. In conjunction with 12th Canadian Infantry Brigade E.21.b.3.6. - E.26.d.3.7. Further advance held up owing to M.G.fire from BEAUFORT and LE QUESNEL high ground. 7th Cavalry Brigade withdrawn from line and concentrated about E.14.d.
	8 p.m. to 9 p.m.	S.O.S. sent up by Infantry and counter attack threatened from direction of BEAUFORT down valley E.21.- Line therefore reinforced and dispositions about 9 p.m. as follows:- 7th Cavalry Brigade E.26. central to E.21.a.9.5. 5th Cavalry Brigade E.21.a.9.5. to E.16.d.7.7. With one Regt in support E.15.a. Line held in conjunction with 11th and 12th Canadian Infantry Brigades. Counter-attack did not materialise and situation remained quiet through the night.
	9 p.m.	Adv. Divl. H.Q. to D.12.c.5.9. W. of CAYEUX W ood.

NARRATIVE.

Date.	Time.	
9th	5 a.m.	7th Cavalry Brigade moved from line to position of readiness about E.14.b. Canadian Cavalry Brigade in reserve near Divl. H.Q. on W. edge of CAYEUX WOOD. Situation quiet all night.
	8 a.m.	Divl. Staff Officer arranged with G.O.C. 11th and 12th Canadian Infantry Brigades for withdrawal of Cavalry from line held during night 8th/9th. Orders issued for Brigades to concentrate in LUCE Valley S. of River between CAIX and CAYEUX and water horses.
	9 a.m.	At request of O.C./Canadian Infantry Battalion 6th Cavalry Brigade left Royals and 6th M.G. Sqdn. 85th in close support of the Brigade until it was clear that attack being carried out by Infantry against "LE QUESNEL at 10 a.m. had made satisfactory progress.
	10 a.m.	Adv. Divl. H.Q. moved to E.1.d.8.3. on CAYEUX - CAIX Road.
	10 to 12 noon.	6th Cavalry Brigade (less 1 Regt and M.G. Sqdn) and 7th Cavalry Brigade concentrated in LUCE Valley F.25. & 26. Canadian Cavalry Brigade in CAYEUX WOOD about D.6.d. & 12.b.
	1.30 p.m.	Royals and 6th M.G's rejoined 6th Cavalry Brigade from Canadian Infantry. Division remained in Corps reserve all day, concentrated as above and with Divl. H.Q. at E.1.d.8.3.
10th	1.30 p.m.	Orders received from Cavalry Corps for 3rd Cavalry Division to cover whole front of Canadian Corps and to take over patrol dispositions of 1st & 2nd Cavalry Divisions, keeping touch with Infantry advance.

MARCH 8TH.

Date Time.	
	Patrols to move out 5 a.m.
	Remainder of Division 5:30 a.m.
2:30 a.m.	Orders issued to 6th Cavalry Brigade to take over patrol dispositions of 2nd Cavalry Division on Front BOUCHOIR - ROUVROY (both inclusive) and to 7th Cavalry Brigade to take over 1st Cavalry Division patrols dispositions on front ROUVROY - ROSIERES-EN-SANTERRE.
5 a.m.	Patrols moved out as above, reporting at 1st Cavalry and 2nd Cavalry Division Headquarters to ascertain dispositions.
5:30 a.m. to 8 a.m.	6th Cavalry Brigade moved from CAYEUX - CAIX Area in LUCE valley through valleys S. of CAIX to a position about E.23.a., 1½ miles West of VRELY. Patrols to WARVILLERS - FOLLIES and ROUVROY in touch with Infantry.
5:30 a.m. to 7:30 a.m.	7th Cavalry Brigade. to E.9.c. valley S. of CAIX, thence to neighbourhood of VRELY. Patrols to North and South of MEHARICOURT in touch with leading Infantry. Canadian Cavalry Brigade to E.13.a. (valley S. of CAIX).
7:10 a.m.	Operation Orders from Canadian Corps received through Cavalry Corps.
7:15 a.m.	Adv Divl. H.Q. to E.16.d. (valley S.E. of CAIX) where situation was explained to G.O.C. Brigades and operation Orders issued instructing Brigades to work on a broad front with Squadrons in close touch with Infantry Advance - Every opportunity to be taken of pushing through and facilitating their further advance.
8 a.m.	Infantry attack commenced.
8:50 a.m.	3rd Cavalry Division disposed as follows:-

NARRATIVE.

Date.	Time.	
		6TH Cavalry Brigade 1½ miles N. of VRELY with patrols in touch with Infantry on general line BOUCHOIR – ROUVROY.
		7th Cavalry Brigade around VRELY with patrols in touch with Infantry N. & S. MEHARICOURT and at CHILLY where they were held up by M.G. fire.
		Canadian Cavalry Brigade M.15.
		Adv. Divl. H.Q. E.16.d.5.5.
	10:30 a.m.	Infantry attacked making progress and 6th Cavalry Brigade moved forward to line BOUCHOIR–FOLLIES– BEAUFORT.
	11 a.m.	1 Company Whippet Tanks sent up to 7th Cavalry Brigade.
	11:30 a.m.	Report received from 32nd Division through 6th Cavalry Brigade that enemy resistance now very weak and that their retirement was rapid.
		Orders issued to 6th Cavalry Brigade to push on as quickly as possible.
		Adv. Divl. H.Q. to E.30.a.2.2.
	12 noon.	32nd Division reported to have taken LA CHAVATTE and FRANSART and possibly FARVILLERS. This report and the information regarding rapid retirement of Infantry proved to be inaccurate. Special patrols sent forward by 7th Cavalry Brigade to report on suitability of ground about line MEHARICOURT – MAUCOURT – FOUQUESCOURT with a view to rapid Cavalry advance.
	12:40 p.m.	Infantry advance making slow progress on 7th Cavalry Brigade front and patrols reported ground in front most unsuitable for Cavalry and impossible to advance except dismounted owing to old trench system, shell holes and wire.

NARRATIVE.

Date.	Time.	
	1 p.m.	Special patrols sent out by 6th Cavalry Brigade to report on suitability of ground on 6th Cavalry Brigade front for rapid advance of Cavalry. Canadian Cavalry Brigade front moved up 6th Cavalry (Brigade front for) to point 2m. w. of WARVILLERS.
	1:10 p.m.	WARVILLERS reported by 6th Cavalry Brigade patrols as still held by the enemy with heavy M.G. cross fire. Our Infantry making slow progress and establisheed on a line 500x N.W. of WARVILLERS. 1 Coy. Whippet Tanks arrived with 6th Cavalry Brigade.
	1:40 p.m.	Patrols reported ground in area ROUVROY-WARVILLERS-LE QUESNOY quite impassable for Cavalry mounted owing to trenches and wire. Tanks Commander also reported it impossible for Whippets.
	1 p.m. to 2 p.m.	In view of strong enemy resistance about WARVILLERS and DAMERY and the necessity for of pushing on, Canadian Cavalry Brigade were ordered to push on and seize high ground N. and N.E. of ROYE. Adv. Davl. H.Q. to R.29.d.4.4. 2m. N. of BEAUFORT. Canadian Cavalry Brigade advanced between BEAUFORT and WARVILLERS but after consultation between G.O.C. Division and G.O.C. 6th Cavalry Brigade regarding the ground and general situation about WARVILLERS and DAMERY it was decided that the only possible line of advance for Canadian Cavalry Brigade was via ROYE Road or South of it.
	3 p.m.	Canadian Cavalry Brigade therefore proceeded via BOUCHOIR and 7th Cavalry Brigade were brought into Divisional support 1 mile west of WARVILLERS. 6th Cavalry Brigade remaining about FOLIES & BOUCHOIR, in position to support Canadian Cavalry Cavalry Brigade.

10.

NARRATIVE.

Date.	Time.	
	4 p.m. to 5 p.m.	Adv. Divl. H.Q. to K.11.c. between FOLIES & BEAUFORT. Canadian Cavalry Brigade in touch with French Infantry attacked and captured ANDECHY, taking 41 Prisoners and a supply dump, including a quantity of rolling stock with supplies on railway. Line was taken up ½ mile East of ANDECHY, but further advance checked by M.G. fire from woods N.E. about DAMERY and Hill 100, and by shell fire from ROYE.
	4.15 p.m.	Three troops Fort Garry Horse then attempted to take Hill 100 (K.10.a) supported by R.C.H.A. Bde. Owing to wire and trenches on either side, a charge down ROYE road was made but attack was beaten off by M.G. fire from Hill 100 – DAMMAY-BOIS-EN-DOMMAY and BOIS-EN-EQUERRE (h.c.b.)
	4.15 p.m.	The Infantry (32nd Division) attacked BOIS-EN-EQUERRE in conjunction with mounted attack of Fort Garry Horse on Hill 100, but could make no progress, the enemy retaining possession of the Wood and a pill box near the Western edge. Casualties to Fort Garry Horse in the charge on Hill 100 were moderately high, but very heavy horse casualties were incurred.
10th.	5.30 p.m.	Situation and Disposition. Canadian Cavalry Brigade. - 2 Squadrons in ANDECHY 2 Regiments South of ROYE Road about 1 mile S.W. of LE QUESNOY - (L.31.a.& K.35.a.) 2 Batteries R.C.H.A. Bde. in action at L.31.a.c. ½ mile S.W. of LE QUESNOY.
	5.30 p.m.	On information which subsequently proved inaccurate that Canadian Cavalry Brigade had taken Hill 100. 6th Cavalry Brigade were ordered to support closely.
	6 p.m.	Situation and Dispositions.

11.

Date.	Time.	NARRATIVE.
		6th Cavalry Brigade.
		2 Regiments 1200 yds West of LE QUESNOY in close support of Canadian Cavalry Brigade.
		1 Regiment (less 1 Sqdn) at LE QUESNOY.
		Remainder of Brigade between FOLLIES and BOUCHOIR.
		7th Cavalry Brigade.
		In Divisional Support between BEAUFORT and CAYVILLERS.
		Divisional Headquarters. K.11.c. on track FOLLIES-BEAUFORT.
	7 p.m.	Orders issued for Brigade to concentrate in bivouac areas for the night between BEAUFORT and FOLLIES.
		Div. H.Q. to E.28.b. 1080 N.W. of BEAUFORT.
	9 p.m.	Brigades concentrated in above bivouac area.
Aug. 11th	a.m.	Division at one hours notice.
	5 p.m.	Division moved Westwards to BOVES area.

3rd Cavalry Division.

NARRATIVE of OPERATIONS, Oct. 8th - 11th, 1918.

Reference 1/40,000 Sheets 57B and 62B.

October 8th.

08:00. In accordance with orders issued, the 3rd Cavalry Division was concentrated by 08:00 in an area S.W. of JONCOURT and S.W. of MAGNY LA FOSSE with Divisional Report Centre on JONCOURT-BELLENGLISE Road ½ mile N. of MAGNY LA FOSSE (H.19.b.)

09:20. 7th Cavalry Brigade, who were ordered to maintain touch with the Brigade (1st Cavalry Brigade) of 1st Cavalry Division moving S. of main ESTREES - LE CATEAU Road so as to protect right rear of that Division in the event of an advance E. of BUSIGNY, moved forward to valley W. of WIANCOURT previously vacated by 1st Cavalry Brigade.

10:/30 Canadian Cavalry Brigade with orders to keep touch with Brigade (2nd Cavalry Brigade) of 1st Cavalry Division moving N. of ESTREES - LE CATEAU Road, moved forward to Valley N. of WIANCOURT (B.22.c. & 23.a) in touch with 2nd Cavalry Brigade. One Regiment was detailed to protect left rear of 1st Cavalry Division as it advanced, remaining two Regiments being in 3rd Cavalry Division Reserve.

10:30 Divisional Report Centre moved to B.22. N.E. of ESTREES on main ESTREES - LE CATEAU Road.

6th Cavalry Brigade in Corps Reserve moved forward to Valley N. of WAINCOURT, sending one Squadron to ESTREES as escort to Cavalry Corps.

11:50 7th Cavalry Brigade, in touch with 1st Cavalry Brigade, moved to Valley S.E. of GENEVE.

Canadian Cavalry Brigade, in touch with 2nd Cavalry Brigade crossed LE CATEAU Road, and moved forward into Valley N.E. of BEAUREVOIR, establishing Report Centre at Farm in C.7.a.

14:30. Reports from 1st Cavalry Division indicated considerable enemy opposition from M.G's along the line of high ground N.E. of SERAIN and Western edge of Woods W. of BUSIGNY.

Patrols from 7th Cavalry Brigade also reported our advanced Cavalry held up by M.Gs. on ridge N.E. of BRANCOURT about FRAICOURT Farm.

16:45. G.C.21 issued, ordering Division back to bivouac for the night in the area MAGNY LA FOSSE - BELLICOURT - NAURCY - JONCOURT.

18:00   Divisional Report Centre moved back for the night to H.19.b on JONCOURT - BELLENGLISE Road.

20:00   Warning Order (G.C. 25) issued that Division would start early tomorrow and be leading Division of Cavalry Corps.

October 9th.

04:00   Conference at Divisional H.Q. and 3rd Cavalry Division Order No. 70 issued.

06:00 to 07:00   In accordance with G.C. 27.
Division concentrated in Valley between BRANCOURT and VAUX LE PRETRE and N. of ESTREES - LE CATEAU Road in U.26.c & C.2.a.

06:00. Divisional Report Centre opened at Farm on ESTREES - LE CATEAU Road C.7.a.

07:10. G.C.31 issued, giving further bounds and objectives beyond LE CATEAU.

08:45. MARETZ reported taken without opposition and touch with retreating enemy had been temporarily lost. 7th Cavalry Brigade were in touch with our advancing Infantry.

09:20. G.O.C. then decided to advance on a two Brigade frontage with 6th Cavalry Brigade on right and Canadian Cavalry Brigade on left, S. and N. of LE CATEAU Road respectively, 7th Cavalry Brigade being brought into Divisional Reserve - G.C.32 issued in confirmation of verbal orders as above.

09:20. Divisional Report Centre established at U.26.d.9.1. (one mile W. of PREMONT).

10:15. 7th Cavalry Brigade were concentrated in Divisional Reserve in Valley 1 mile W. of PREMONT in accordance with above order.

10:00

3.

10:00 to 11:00

(a) 6th Cavalry Brigade advanced guard reported our Infantry held up by M.G. fire from the Railway 1 mile S.E. of HONNECHY, and a Squadron was sent forward through V.3. about a mile N. of BUSIGNY to turn the position from the Sth. Wired enclosures E. of the Railway, however, rendered a mounted advance impracticable.

Another Squadron was then ordered to work round through V.9. further South, but this order was cancelled on receipt of information that Infantry was about to attack.

The main body of 6th Cavalry Brigade were ordered up to Valley just E. of MARETZ.

(b) The Canadian Cavalry Brigade found the Infantry held up by M.G. fire from the line Western edge of BOIS DE GATTIGNY to CLARY.

A Squadron of the F.G.H. was therefore sent forward against the Western edge of the BOIS DE GATTIGNY, covered on the left flank by the L.S.H. who were ordered to seize the Wood at the S. end of CLARY (O.23.d.) and the high ground to the East of that village, the whole advance being covered by M.Gs. and 1 Battery of the R.C.H.A. Brigade.

By 11:10 the F.G.H. had captured the W. edge of BOIS DE GATTIGNY and the advance Squadron of L.S.H. was established on the high ground N.E. of CLARY (O.18) The enemy still held that portion of the BOIS bordering on the main MAUROIS - MARETZ Road but abandoned this on the Infantry attacking.

In the above operation 230 prisoners, 1 5.9" How., 2 Field guns and 30 or 40 M.Gs. were taken by L.S.H. and F.G.H.

11:30 to 12:00

SITUATION 6th Cavalry Brigade in Valley E. of MARETZ with patrols in touch with Infantry about P.28.d. near S. exit of HONNECHY and advanced Squadron about P.33.b.

Heavy M.G. fire from HONNECHY.

Canadian Cavalry Brigade. on line CLARY, which was clear of enemy, through the BOIS DE GATTIGNY to Wood in P.20.d where they were held up by M.G. fire from HONNECHY.

7th Cavalry Brigade in Divisional Reserve and assembled

in Valley S. of MARETZ.

Divisional Report Centre on main road 500 yards S.W. of MARETZ (U.11.d.9.9.) wither it had moved at 11:00.

12:00 to 12:30

In consultation with G.Os.C. 6th and Canadian Cavalry Brigades, G.O.C. division decided to encircle HONNECHY from the South with 6th Cavalry Brigade who were to seize as objective the high ground in P.23.a. N.E. of that place, whilst the Canadian Cavalry Brigade moved N. of MAUROIS to seize the high ground P.16.d joining up the 6th Cavalry Brigade. If opportunity offered, a further advance was to be made N.E. of REUMONT to the line Q.13.d. – P.5.d.

13:00 to 15:00

Infantry had arranged to attack HONNECHY about 14:00 and 6th Cavalry Brigade sent one Regiment (3rd D.G.) with two armoured forward in conjunction with this attack from direction of BUSIGNY to seize high ground P.23.a., one Regiment (Royals) attacking simultaneously on their left.

Inniskilling Dragoons temporarily placed at disposal of 6th Cavalry Brigade from 7th Cavalry Brigade were to advance to P.35. in echelon to right rear of 3rd Dragoon Guards.

The attack as above ordered commenced at 14:00 and by 14:40 HONNECHY was captured by 3rd Dragoon Guards and the high ground in P.23. occupied in spite of heavy shell fire and M.G. fire from BOIS de PROYART and ESCAUFORT. The Royal Dragoons had attacked at the same time through P.28. and 22 N. of MAUROIS. In the meantime the Canadian Cavalry Brigade had captured MAUROIS, taking 40 prisoners and 3 M.Gs. just North of the village. Further to the North, between BERTRY and CLARY 42 prisoners and 5 M.Gs. were also taken by Canadian Cavalry Brigade. The Brigade, were, however, now held up on the MAUROIS-BERTRY Road by heavy M.G. fire from REUMONT and the high ground N. of HONNECHY.

15:00 to 16:30

One Squadron Canadian Cavalry Brigade were therefore ordered forward to seize high ground N. of REUMONT passing to the left of the Regiment (F.G.H.) on the MAUROIS-BERTRY Road and gaining touch with the left Regiment (L.S.H.) of the Brigade near BERTRY. A second Squadron was ordered to swing round on a smaller circle and seize the N.W. end of REUMONT, whilst two more Squadrons attacked along the road.

L.S.H. on the left were ordered to clear BERTRY and push forward to TROISVILLES so as to protect left flank. This operation was covered by the fire of R.C.H.A. Brigade and a 4.5 How. Battery from the valley W. of MAUROIS and all available machine guns, and eventually resulted in the capture of the line E. exit of REUMONT-LA SOTIERE at the N.E. exit of TROISVILLES. One Officer and 29 O.R. and 3 M.Gs. were captured as they retired from REUMONT and a number of the enemy killed with the sword. During this operation, a report was received that numerous guns and transport were retiring down the INCHY-LE CATEAU Road and the L.S.H. were therefore ordered to push on beyond TROISVILLES across this road, fire from 4.5 How Battery being directed on it.

15:00 to 16:00

Meanwhile the 6th Cavalry Brigade on the right had ordered one Regiment (K.R.H.) forward to seize spur E. and S.E. of REUMONT and One Regiment (Inniskilling) to advance on ST.BENIN keeping S. of R. des ESSARTS.

REUMONT was however still held and the enemy offered strong resistance on the line ST. SOUPLET-REUMONT.

16:00

6th Cavalry Brigade ordered to push on at once towards LE CATEAU to deny roads running East from that town to the enemy who had been seen retiring through it.

Owing to being involved in action against the line ST. SOUPLET-REUMONT, 6th Cavalry Brigade were not able to carry out the above task.

(See B.M. 30 cancelled by B.M.32).

17:00

G.C. 46 was therefore issued ordering 7th Cavalry Brigade to pass W. and N. of HONNECHY and MAUROIS and to push on in conjunction with Canadian Cavalry Brigade to carry out mission allotted 6th Cavalry Brigade in G.H.10.

17:30.

6th Cavalry Brigade were concentrated in P.17.d. ready to support 7th Cavalry Brigade and Canadian Cavalry Brigade.

17:45.	7th Cavalry Brigade moving W. and N. of MAUROIS into position in touch with Canadian Cavalry Brigade just N.E. of REUMONT, with one Squadron as advanced guard holding high ground overlooking LE CATEAU (Q.1.c. and Q.7.a) and connecting up with 6th and Canadian Cavalry Brigades.
17:30. to 18:00	Canadian Cavalry Brigade ordered one Regiment (R.C.D.) forward to seize final objective between MONTAY and RAMB CURLIEUX Farm, left Regiment (L.S.H.) to continue line from RAMBOURLIEUX Farm to TROISVILLES.

F.G.H. came into Brigade reserve, R.C.D. having passed through them.

By this time it was quite dark and further appreciable advance was not practicable.

18:00   SITUATION.

6th Cavalry Brigade held a line of posts and M.Gs. N.E. and S.E. of REUMONT to HONNECHY (inclusive).

7th Cavalry Brigade assembled in N. of REUMONT with one Squadron in advance about Q.1.c. and 7.a. maintaining touch with 6th Cavalry Brigade on right and Canadian Cavalry Brigade on left.

Canadian Cavalry Brigade holding line from high ground 500 yards S.W. of MONTAY (about K.27.b.) through K.20 to X-roads N.W. of RAMBOURLIEUX Farm, thence along road to LA SOTIERE (J.29.d.)

Patrols entered MONTAY and worked along Southern MONTAY-NEUVILLY Road. Patrols also entered NEUVILLY.

Owing to exposed right flank between LE CATEAU and REUMONT one Regiment (F.G.H.) less one Squadron were pushed forward to about PONT DES 4 VAUX, patrols to LE CATEAU and in touch with Regiment on left near MONTAY.

Divisional Report Centre P.27.a.- S.W. of MAUROIS.

18:15.   XVIII Corps Cyclists arrived to take over line from 6th Cavalry Brigade round REUMONT. (See G.C. 31 from Cavalry Corps)

Division ordered to bivouac for the night in position captured or withdrawn after relief by Infantry.

18:30.   Divisional Report Centre moved to P.26.b.3.0.(BOIS DE GATTIGNY) for the night.

21:00   G.O.55 issued ordering Division to be ready to move 06:00 tomorrow 10th October.

CASUALTIES.

6th Cavalry Brigade.

Officers	2 Killed
"	11 Wounded
O.R.	14 Killed
"	134 Wounded
Horses.	255

Canadian Cavalry Brigade.

Officers	2 Killed
"	10 Wounded
O.R.	28 Killed
"	101 Wounded
Horses.	171.

October 10th.

00:15.   Cavalry Corps order No. 70 received, and

01:15   3rd Cavalry Division Order No. 71 issued.

06:00   Divisional Report Centre established at P.4.b.5.0. S. exit of TROISVILLES.

7th Cavalry Brigade passed through line held by Canadian Cavalry Brigade with objective high ground FOREST-AMERVAL. (L.7. to K.4. cent.) patrols being sent to LE CATEAU-MONTAY-NEUVILLY.

Canadian Cavalry Brigade withdrew to valley S. of TROISVILLES

6th Cavalry Brigade assembled in Valley N.W. of REUMONT.

07:30   Patrols sent out by 7th Cavalry Brigade reported heavy shell and Machine Gun fire from N.W. corner of LE CATEAU and MONTAY and from N.E. of River SELLE.

NEUVILLY also reported strongly held by enemy with Machine Guns one Squadron coming under direct fire about RAMBOURLIEUX Farm.

07:45.   One Regiment (Inniskillings) occupied high ground overlooking

INCHY-LE CATEAU Road (K.32.-K.25). One Squadron in advance being compelled to retire to above line by heavy fire from N. of SELLE VALLEY.

Patrols sent out to reconnoitre N. of NEUVILLY.

Infantry also reported heavy shell fire on slopes W. of MONTAY.

08:30   One Brigade of Artillery (33rd Division) and 5 Armoured Cars sent forward to assist advance of 7th Cavalry Brigade.

09:00   Owing to heavy shell and Machine Gun fire with direct observation by enemy along line of River SELLE from LE CATEAU to NEUVILLY (both inclusive) 7th Cavalry Brigade were ordered to withdraw out of observation and to send reconnaissance esto BRIASTRE with a view to crossing River SELLE at that point.

09:30. 7th Cavalry Brigade withdrew to position in Valley E. of TROISVILLES out of direct observation.

Patrol working N. of NEUVILLY met with heavy Machine Gun fire from N.W. corner of that village and were also fired on from VIESLY, which was strongly held.

11:00   Situation unchanged.

Reports received through 7th Cavalry Brigade that enemy were retiring in large numbers E. of FOREST on LE CATEAU-MAUBEUGE Road but out of range of Field Artillery. Cavalry Corps informed and asked to turn on heavy guns.

14:15. Cavalry Corps G.C.45. received.

G.C.69 issued, ordering Division back to bivouac for night as follows:-

6th and Canadian Cavalry Brigades about MONTIGNY.

7th Cavalry Brigade just W. of BERTRY.

Divisional Troops and Divisional H.Q. to MONTIGNY.

17:15. Divisional Report Centre established on CLARY-CAUDRY Road (O.11.d.5.5.) just S. of MONTIGNY with Brigades and Divisional Troops as afore-mentioned.

19:15. Division ordered to be saddled up and ready to move at 08:30 tomorrow (11th) (G.C.72).

20:30. Division at 1 hour's notice from 08:00 Tomorrow, 11th.

CASUALTIES.

                7th Cavalry Brigade. (October 9th and 10th).

Officers.   9 Wounded.

O.R.   11 Killed.

"   73 Wounded.

Horses.   131.

October 11th.

12:15.   3rd Cavalry Division order No. 72 issued, 6th Cavalry Brigade being ordered to bivouac area in ELINCOURT, to relieve congestion in MONTIGNY.

12:30.   Division at 4 hour's notice.

            A.1. and A.2. Echelons rejoined Brigades etc.

18:35.   6th Cavalry Brigade completed move to ELINCOURT.

            Divisional Report Centre remained at O.11.d.5.8. MONTIGNY.

                            Major General,
                    Commanding 3rd Cavalry Division.

15th October. 1918.

6th CAVALRY BRIGADE.

NARRATIVE OF OPERATIONS, October 9th, 1918.

Note. This narrative only gives the situation as known to Brigade H.Q. from the information available at the time decisions were made.

01:50. G.O.C. and B.M. ordered to attend Conference at Divl H.Q.

04:00. Brigade ordered to be concentrated in B.12.a. and b.(Sheet 62B)

04:00. 3rd C.D. order No. 70 received at Conference. Brigade ordered to advance in Echelon on right of 7th Cav. Bde. with objective spurs overlooking valley between LE CATEAU and ST BENIN.

07:00. Bds. concentrated in C.18.b. with H.Q. at C.13.d.1.1.
1 Field Troop joined Brigade.
B.M. 12 (Operation Order) issued to all units.

07:10. G.C.31 received (continuation of C.O.70 in event of success), and issued verbally to C.O's.

08:20. G.O.C. and Brigade Major ordered to meet Divisional Commander C.2. cent.

08:35. Brigade ordered up to C.2.b. at a trot, as our Infantry were reported to be 1½ miles in front of MARETZ, and touch had been lost with 7th Cavalry Brigade, who were advanced guard to Division.

09:00. Brigadier saw Commanding Officers at C.2.cent, and ordered Royals to act as advanced guard to Brigade, and move at once parallel to and S. of the Main LE CATEAU Road with Objectives as given in B.M.12; 10th Hussars to follow Royals, detailing one Squadron as right flank guard.
Liaison Officer was despatched to keep touch with Canadian Cavalry Brigade, who were advancing on our left.

09:50. Royals were seen to have crossed the MARETZ-BUSIGNY Road.

10:05. Patrols reported BUTRY Farm held by enemy, and our Infantry attacking it.

10:30	Advanced Squadron reported our Infantry held up by Machine Gun fire from Railway P.28.c and P.34.a.
	Squadron sent to high ground in V.3.cent., to turn the position from the South.
	There was, however, too much wire just east of the Railway for a mounted advance to be feasible.
11:00.	10th Hussars were ordered to send a Squadron to work round N. of Railway in V.9.
	This order was subsequently cancelled, on receipt of information that our Infantry in V.4. were going to attack.
11:10.	Main body of Brigade ordered to V.1.b.
12:00.	Royals were now about P.32.c. with advanced Squadron at P.33.b.
	Patrols in touch with Infantry, who were now on high ground at P.28.d. and meeting strong Machine Gun opposition from HONNECHY.
13:05.	The Brigade, less Royals and Brigade H.Q' was withdrawn behind the MARETZ-BUSIGNY Road, owing to heavy shelling of the ground N.E. of it.
	Brigade Intelligence Officer reported that his O.P. was established at Railway Junction P.34.c.0.8. at 11:40 and our Infantry were along stream in V.4.
12:15.	Brigadier met G.O's.C. 3rd Cavalry Division and Canadian Cavalry Brigade at V.1.b.1.8.
	It was decided that if HONNECHY was taken by our Infantry, or an opportunity occurred for an advance, 6th and Canadian Cavalry Brigades were to seize the high ground P.23.a.-P.16.cent and then push on and seize the high ground Q.13.d.-P.5.d.; 6th Cavalry Brigade to move S. of HONNECHY and Canadian Cavalry Brigade N. of MAUROIS.
13:00	B.M. 19 issued ordering Royals to advance if opportunity occurred.
	During the Conference at 12:15 reports were issued received from Brigade I.O. and Royals Advanced Squadron, to the effect that the enemy was holding the high ground P.34.a. and P.35.b.

3.

...strongly, and that situation in BUSIGNY and LA SABLIERE WOOD was not yet cleared up.

13:15. Reports from Royals and Brigade O.P. showed that the ground would only permit of a _rapid_ advance on HONNECHY from two directions, the road from MARETZ or the road from BUSIGNY.

Royals and Brigade O.P. reported that Infantry were going to have 5 minutes bombardment at 13:55, and then attempt to advance on HONNECHY and South of it.

G.O.C.39 received from 3rd Cavalry Division that armoured cars reported that they had been through HONNECHY and MAUROIS.

In view of other information in possession, this was considered very unlikely, and subsequently proved to be quite untrue.

13:25. G.O.C. decided to send 3rd Dragoon Guards with 2 armoured cars to seize the high ground at P.23.e. from the direction of BUSIGNY.

This attack to take place at 14:00, and Royals were ordered to advance simultaneously on their left.

13:45. Inniskillings were placed at disposal of G.O.C. 6th Cavalry Brigade and were ordered to advance in echelon to right rear of 3rd Dragoon Guards and seize spur in P.35. (B.M.21.)

13:55. Barrage arranged by Infantry did not come down, as they had seen signs of enemy retirement and cancelled it.

14:10. 3rd Dragoon Guards advanced from North of BUSIGNY, under heavy enfilade M.G. fire from ESCAUFORT and B. PROYART.

Royals advanced simultaneously through P.28. P.22 and North of MAUROIS.

This advance was made under considerable shell fire, and very heavy M.G. fire from a large number of E.A.

14:30. Report received that Canadian Cavalry Brigade had captured MAUROIS, and handed it over to Infantry, and were pushing on to N.E. of REUMONT.

14:40. 3rd Dragoon Guards captured HONNECHY, and high ground P.23.c. Brigade H.Q. established P.28.cent. Advanced H.Q.

              moving to HONNECHY.

15:25.   G.O.C. decided to send 10th Hussars on to spur in Q.13.c and d. and Inniskillings South of River towards St. BENIN.

15:40.   B.M. 26 despatched to Inniskillings by Liaison Officer giving orders accordingly.

15:45.   Canadian Cavalry Brigade B.X.28 timed 15:05, received saying that enemy held REUMONT.

16:00.   "C" Battery ordered to HONNECHY.

    HONNECHY and the ground round it was heavily shelled ever since it was captured, and 3rd Dragoon Guards had suffered heavy casualties from this and from Machine Gun fire during their advance.

16:22.   The situation, as known at Brigade H.Q. was that enemy held REUMONT and a line running down the St SOUPLET Road.

    This was reported to Divisional H.Q. (B.M.280 and tanks were asked for to clear REUMONT.

16:30.   Inniskillings reported (16:05) that one Squadron was at P.35.a. and other two coming up.

16:30.   G.H.10 received from 3rd Cavalry Division ordering Brigade to push on at once as enemy had been seen retiring through LE CATEAU.

    At this time the only troops in hand were one Squadron 10th Hussars holding E. edge of HONNECHY dismounted (which had been put in to save 3rd Dragoon Guards more horse casualties) and half the machine gun squadron who were in with them.

    Royals were between MAUROIS and REUMONT, and 3rd Dragoon Guards very scattered owing to patrols and casualties.

16:40.   G.O.C. informed Division of this and recommended that the two fresh Regiments of 7th Cavalry Brigade should be sent forward.

16:50.   3rd Dragoon Guards reported REUMONT now clear, and Royals were reported to be assembled S.W. of it.

    10th Hussars were also in hand, and G.O.C. therefore decided to push on at once.

17:00.   O.Cs. 10th Hussars and Royals given verbal orders, and 3rd

Cavalry Division informed of this decision (B.M.30).

17:05. B.M.31 despatched to Inniskillings, ordering them to move West of St BENIN to high ground South of LE CATEAU and interrupt Railway about Q.5.b.; if unable to advance past ESCAUFORT, to move through HONNECHY, MAUROIS, and REUMONT and join 7th Cavalry Brigade.

17:18. Brigade H.Q. established in P.18.c.

Message from Inniskillings, timed 16:30, that two Sqdns had been diverted N. of HONNECHY to join 7th Cavalry Bdge.; the other one would remain in P.35.a. to cover right flank of 6th Cavalry Brigade.

Message from Royals, timed 16:10, received, reporting capture of REUMONT, and that Canadian Cavalry Brigade did not appear to have made progress beyond squares P.10 and 16.

17:30. The Brigade was now ready to move on final objectives, and Royals were just starting, when G.C.46 was received from 3rd Cavalry Division that 7th Cavalry Brigade had been ordered to take final objective.

Division were therefore informed, both by visual and galloper, that the Brigade was assembled in P.17.d. and ready to support 7th Cavalry Brigade closely.

17:50. A line of posts and machine guns was established from HONNECHY to REUMONT, both inclusive.

Heavy Machine Gun fire continued from East of REUMONT and there was considerable shelling with H.E. and Blue Cross.

A low flying enemy aeroplane succeeded in dropping two bombs on Squadron of 10th Hussars, wounding 4 Officers and a number of men, and killing a lot of horses.

17:55. Brigade H.Q. established P.17.c.7.8. and Brigade scattered about in P.17.c. and d.

18:15. XVIII Corps Cyclists arrived at Brigade H.Q. and O.C. reported that he had been ordered to take over the line from 6th Cavalry Brigade. This was started at once.

19:05. Following order was issued:-

B.M.35.   9   AAA

"XVIII Corps Cyclists are taking over our line AAA As soon as relieved units will water and off-saddle AAA B Squadron 7th D.G. will be in support to the left Sector, i.e. up to BOIS FME, inclusive AAA Royals will be in support to the remainder of the line i.e. up to HONNECHY AAA 3 D.G. and X.R.H. will be in reserve AAA Brigade H.Q. at P.17.c.7.8.

       6 Cav. Bde.   19:05

19:15. Brigadier rode to Divisional H.Q. to report on days operations.

23:00. Warning order received to be ready to move at 06:00 hours on 10th.

  Quiet night.

      (sgd) D.D.WALLACE, Captain.
      Brigade Major 6th Cavalry Brigade.
11th October 1918.

APPENDIX II.

Narrative of Operations of 6th Dismounted Brigade.
March 21st - 27th. 1918.

March 21st. Left DEVISE 4:45 p.m. 3rd Cavalry Division marched to BEAUMONT. (30 miles.)

March 22nd. At 2 a.m. 6th Dismounted Brigade was formed, under Lieut. Colonel A. Burt, D.S.O. 3rd Dragoon Guards.

Strength.

3rd Dragoons Guards.	180)	
1st Royal Dragoons.	180)	approximately.
10th Royal Hussars.	120)	
6th M.G. Squadron.	60)	

and proceeded by bus from UGNEY to VIRY NOUREUIL, arriving at 4:30 a.m. coming under orders of 173rd Infantry Brigade. (Brig. General Worgan, 58th Division.)

A trench line, partly dug, was taken up between VIRY NOUREUIL and NOUREUIL. Headquarters at NOUREUIL. 3rd Dragoon Guards on the right with 14th Pioneer Battalion on Sth. Flank; Royals in centre and 10th Hussars on left; with a Detachment of 3rd London Regiment and 14th Division (Bedford Regiment) on their left.

Day spent in improving trenches and putting up wire.

March 23rd. Following on a counter-attack made by 133rd French Regiment on TERGNIER and the BUTTS, the Germans delivered a fresh attack with overwhelmed the counter-attacks and broke through in masses at the BUTTS. Another force through further North and rapidly arrived at N.N.E. entrance of NOUREUIL on our extreme left Iflank. The Cavalry Line, which was attacked twice in various parts, maintained its position, and Officers of the 2nd and 3rd London Regiment and 6th Dismounted Brigade Headquarters rallied troops falling back, throwing out a defensive flank and holding on to the village till dark.

March 24th. The 6th Dismounted Brigade received orders from the 58th Division to withdraw to a line about CHAUNY. This was done without incident, although the Germans were only 100 yards distant in the outskirts of the Village and to the West of it. At 3:30 a.m. a line was taken up in the Sunk Road running north from CHAUNY with details of the London Regt. and Oxford Hussars on the right and French troops (133rd) on left. Germans attacked at 8:30 a.m. under cover of mist. They advaced up to 20 yards, speaking English, and were driven back by Hotchkiss and rifle fire. About 9:30 a.m. the mist lifted, and it was found that the French had moved back. The order was received to move to ABBECOURT. This had to be done over open Country under very heavy Machine Gun fire, as the Germans had advanced round CHAUNY on the right and forced the French back on the left.

The night was spent at MANICAMP lining the Canal.

March 25th. At 9:30 a.m. ordered by Colonel Commanding French Divn. (Colonel Pichat) to move to high ground South of QUIERZY. To carry out this movement, an Officer was sent to the head of the Column and directed it to a position immediately outside QUIERZY, where it came under heavy shell fire. The Column therefore moved across the open to a position at LES BRUYERS.

At About 12 noon, an order was received from the Brigade (173rd) to re-occupy QUIERZY, and at the same time instructio were received only to take orders from our own Brigadier. Units in this area had been at first placed under orders of the French, but dual control had started, and the scheme proved unworkable.

QUIERZY was occupied by half the Dismounted Brigade, the remainder being held in reserve.

The Bridges over the Canal had been blown up, and the one over the River was burning.

March 26th. Relieved by London Regiments and marched to BESME, arriving there at 6 a.m. The Brigadier, 173rd Infantry Brigade expressed his satisfaction at the way the work had been carried out.

At 3 p.m. marched to TRACY-LE-MONT on the way being

inspected by Major General Cator (G.O.C. 58th Division) who issued a letter expressing his great appreciation of the work carried out by the 6th Dismounted Brigade.

March 27th.   At 11 a.m. horses were sent to meet the 6th Dismounted Brigade, which broke up and joined their respective Units at CHOISY-AU-BAC.

APPENDIX III.

Action of 3rd Cavalry Division at VILLESELVE.

At 8:30 a.m. 24th March, received orders at BERLANCOURT to push forward in the direction of OUGNY insupport of Disorganised Infantry. On reaching VILLESELVE Infantry line had broken. Cavalry was pushed forward and line re-established from BEAUMONT to neighbourhood of EAUCOURT. Were ordered to withdraw to support the 9th French Division but Infantry line again broke on withdrawal of Cavalry. General Harman issued orders to return to restore situation. The 7th and Canadian Brigades were sent mounted around the Southern side of VILLESELVE and established a line from BEAUMONT which was the left of the French position, to the road junction ½ mile N.W. of BEAULIEU. The 6th Brigade under Major Williams was sent through COLLEZY with instructions to charge through the German line, then swing right handed in a N.W. direction along their line, using the sword only.

The detachment moved along the main road to VILLESELVE, taking the Sunken Track running North into COLLEZY. On approaching COLLEZY, it came under M.G. fire from direction of GOLANCOURT, but got under cover of a big farm at S.E. exit of village.

The Detachment was formed into 3 troops by regiments, 3rd Dragoon Guards under Lieut. VINCENT forming 1st wave, 10th Hussars under Major Williams 2nd wave, Royals under Capt. Turner 3rd wave.

The attack was carried out in "Infantry attack" formation the first two waves in line extended, the 3rd wave in sections but covering the flanks of 2 leading waves.

The 3rd Dragoon Guards moved in the direction of COPSE A encountering some German Infantry who were either killed or captured. Some of the enemy ran into the Copse where they were followed on foot and many shot at point blank range in the back as they ran away. 12 Prisoners were handed over to the Infantry by 3rd Dragoon Guards.

Major Williams led the 10th Hussars and Royals on the West side of COPSE A, where the greater part of the hostile Infantry were posted. All three Regiments were under M.G. fire for about 1000 yards (the last 200 yards was over plough), but when within 200 yards of the enemy the latter bearing the men cheering, surrendered freely. The 10th Hussars rode straight through the enemy. The Royals followed and mopped up small parties who had run together after the 10th had passed through them.

After the melee, "Rally" was sounded, prisoners collected wounded picked up, and the Squadron returned to the main BERLANCOURT VILLESELVE road. 94 Prisoners were brought in by 10th Hussars and Royals, making a total of 106 in all. One M.G. was brought back intact and two others put out of action.

Besides the 106 prisoners, taken, between 70 and 100 of the enemy were sabred. The losses of the Detachment were 73 out of 150, but the manoeuvre gave the Infantry renewed confidence and they pushed forward to a line running from the outskirts of GOLANCOURT almost to EAUCOURT, including Hill 81. The re-established enabled the remnants of 2 Battalions which had been fighting near CUGNY to retire on VILLESELVE, at which point they were re-established and sent back into the line.

French troops came up and the mounted Detachment of the 3rd Cavalry Division withdrew to a support line across the main road ¾ mile S.W. of VILLESELVE. Orders were then received that the French having decided to take up a new line near GUISCARD the Cavalry was to cover the retirement of the Infantry to that point and then withdrew to MUIRANCOURT. This was done successfully.

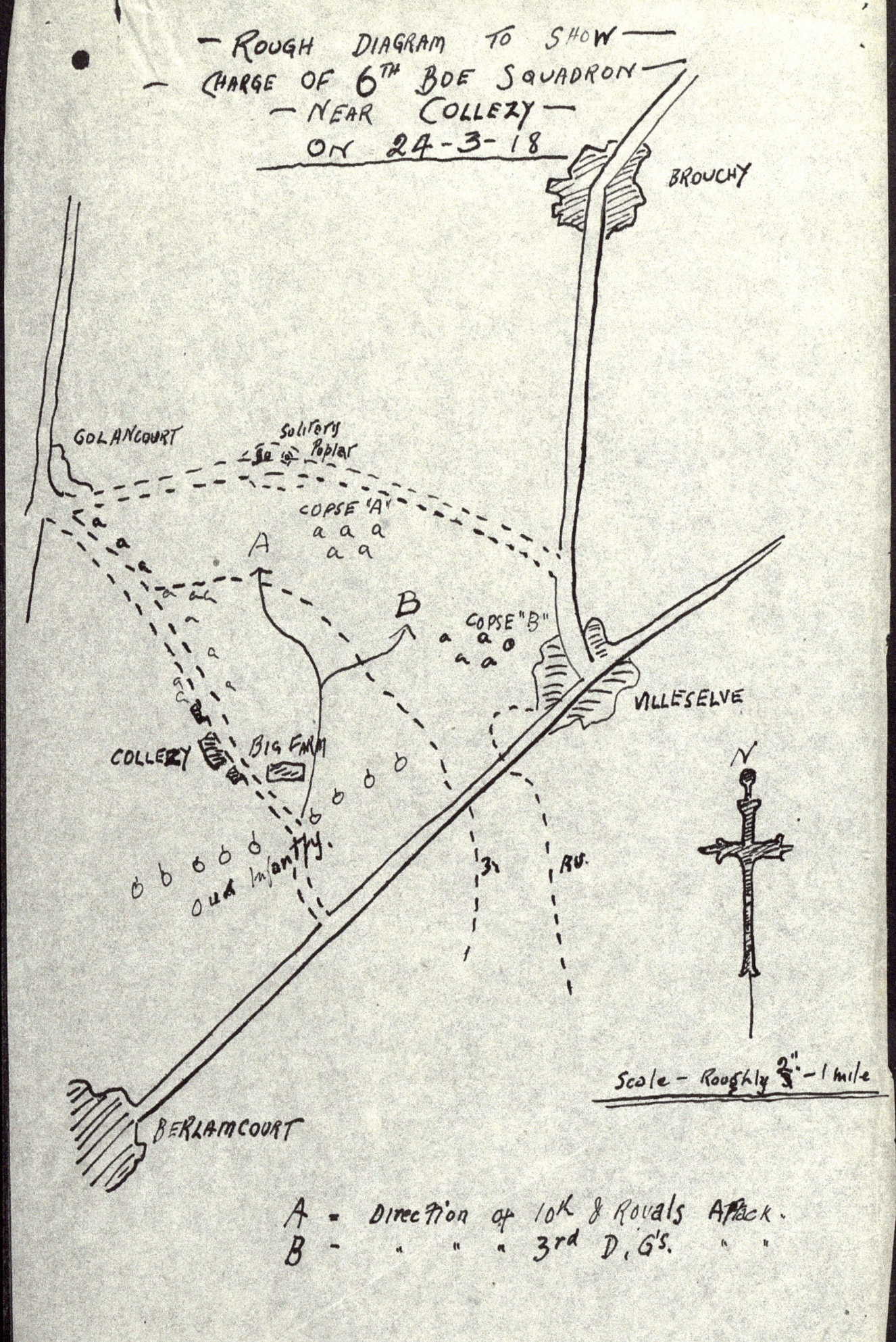

APPENDIX. IV.

Narrative of Operations of Brigadier General Portal's
Detachment.   March 26th - 27th.

March 26th.

7:30 a.m.   Details of 3rd Cavalry Division consisting of 650
other ranks and 3rd Field Squadron R.E. concentrated
at LES CLOYES. 1 patrol of 100 other ranks 7th Cavalry
Brigade was sent to PONTOISE, and 1 patrol of 100 other
ranks Canadian Cavalry Brigade to SEMPIGNY, to remain in
observation in those places. Standing patrol (6 O.R.)
sent to OURSCAMP. Liaison Officers sent to 18th Division
at CAISNES and to 2nd Cavalry Division at CHIRY.

9:0 a.m.   Patrols reports :-

(a) French Dismounted Cavalry holding the front line
from BRETIGNY - PONTOISE. Both bridges at VARESNES
destroyed. Those at PONTOISE prepared for demolition.

(b) Enemy advancing on NOYON - SEMPIGNY Road, 2 kms.
North of Canal. French troops holding SEMPIGNY. Bridge
over the Canal prepared for demolition.

9:20 a.m.   Bridges over OISE and Canal at SEMPIGNY reported
destroyed. French troops holding S. Bank of Canal VARESNES
to Mt. RENAUD.

9:30 a.m.   3rd Dismounted Division (less 6th Dismounted Brigade)
joined the Detachment mounted.

10:15 a.m.   Detachment ordered to move via OURSCAMP to support 2nd
Cavalry Division in attack on high ground in I.22.b., 16.b.,
10.a., (sheet 70.E.)

11:0 a.m.   Above order cancelled. Detachment to remain in Corps
Reserve.

1:40 p.m.   Right patrol reported that French had withdrawn to
South Bank of River OISE and partially blown up Bridges
at PONTOISE.

2:35 p.m.   Left patrol reported enemy attack developing against
French at Mt. RENAUD. Situation at SEMPIGNY quiet.

March 27th.

9:0 a.m.   Morning report - situation quiet. Received orders for Canadian Cavalry Brigade to move with 2nd Cavalry Division to Fifth Army Area.

11:0 a.m.   Received orders for remainder of Detachment (less 1 Squadron) to concentrate at CHOISY. "B" Squadron Iniskilling Dragoons left at LES CLOYES as contact Squadron to protect left flank of 18th Division and keep III Corps informed of the situation.

APPENDIX V.

Action of Harman's Force.
March 26th - BOIS DES ESSARTS.

On the 26th, orders were received for the 3rd Cavalry Division Detachment to push the enemy out of the BOIS DES ESSARTS and Mt. De PORQUERICOURT in I.9.central where they had obtained a footing, and connect up from Fme. CHARBONNEAUX in I.1.b. to Pitman's Force in the neighbourhood of DIVES LE FRANC. This was done successfully, the attack being made by the Canadian Brigades and a portion of the 7th Cavalry Brigade Dismounted, the remainder of the 6th and 7th Cavalry Brigades protecting the right flank by holding the BOIS DE LA RESERVE. Touch was obtained with Pitman's Force at road junction in I.15.central and with the 2nd Cavalry Division at edge of BOIS DES ESSARTS in I.2.d., thus establishing a line from North of DIVES LE FRANC to LAGNY. After connecting with Pitman's Force, the 6th Cavalry Brigade were withdrawn to a position in support in the neighbourhood of Detachment Headquarters at the Chateau in I.13.b.9.7. and direct communication was opened along the main road through GUY to Harman's Detachment at DIVES.

The Northumberland Hussars which had been attached to the Canadian Brigade were detached to come under the command of Colonel Cook, 2nd Cavalry Division, and hold the high ground at Eastern end of Montagne De LAGNY. Later, the enemy, who had crossed at CATIGNY, broke through the French Line in the neighbourhood of CANDON and turned the left flank of the 2nd Cavalry Division who were compelled to retire on DIVES. Col. Cook was killed at this time.

This left the left flank of the 3rd Cavalry Mounted Detachment exposed at the edge of the Wood in I.2.d.

The 6th Cavalry Brigade Detachment were ordered to push forward mounted in the direction of Fme CHARBONNEAUX to support the 2nd Cavalry Division and were the last troops to withdraw. Colonel Stevenson of the Canadian Brigade was sent to draw the left flank in the BOIS DES ESSARTS, and all horses of the 3rd Cavalry Detachment were sent back through GUY under Captain Parbury of the 17th Lancers.

Word was passed to Pitman's Force of the situation and that the 3rd Cavalry Division Detachment would protect his left flank. The latter fought a rear guard action on foot gradually retiring on GUY, at which point a determined stand was made which delayed the enemy sufficiently to enable the 6th Cavalry Brigade Detachment to get clear and Pitman's Force to withdraw on DIVES LE FRANC. This action was continued over the BOIS DE LA RESERVE and BOIS DE CLOCHETTES, the 3rd Cavalry Detachment ultimately crossing the river at EVRICOURT and H.23.b.7.0., where the horses were waiting and where the French had put a line across the river. At this point orders were received to retire to ELINCOURT which was reached about 10 p.m. on the 26th.

APPENDIX VI.

Narrative of Operations - Canadian Cavalry Brigade.
(A) Capture of BOIS DE MOREUIL   March 30th.
(B) Capture of RIFLE WOOD.   April 1st.

Aa.

At 2 p.m. on March 29th the Canadian Cavalry Brigade received orders to march to JUMEL. During the march orders were received to proceed to GUYENCOURT, where the Brigade bivouacked in GUYENCOURT Wood. The Brigade stood to at dawn on March 30th, having received orders at 2 a.m. to be ready to move at 6:30 a.m. The hour to move was postponed until 8:30 a.m. at which hour the G.O.C. men General Pitman, Commanding 2nd Cavalry Division, who gave him the following information and orders:-   The Germans had captured MEZIERES and were advancing rapidly towards AMIENS. The Brigade was to cross the NOYE and the AVRE Rivers as quickly as possible and engage and delay the enemy.

Orders were issued accordingly to move at once across country from REMIENCOURT, leaving BOIS DE SENCAT on the right and endeavour to force a crossing at CASTEL. The crossing at CASTEL was unopposed and the Brigade proceeded due East to the Northern extremity of the BOIS DE MOREUIL. At that point considerable machine guns and rifle fire was encountered coming from the Northern face of the Wood. It was apparent that the retention of this wood by the enemy, giving them direct observation on the whole of the Valley leading up to AMIENS might be fatal to AMIENS, and the G.O.C. accordingly decided to attack and take the Wood.

Headquarters were established at the Northern edge of the small wood adjoining the large one. This small wood had not yet been occupied by the enemy. The Royal Canadian Dragoons, who were leading were ordered to send an advance-guard Squadron commanded by Capt. Nordheimer at a gallop to clear the North-Western corner of the wood, the 2nd Squadron, commanded by Capt. Newcomen, also mounted, to the S.W. face of the wood.

with the object if possible of gaining touch with Major Timmis'
Squadron at the extreme southern corner of the wood, the 3rd
Squadron commanded by Major Timmis' was ordered to gallop
round the N.E. corner of the wood up to the Southern corner.
Capt. Nordheimer's Squadron, although exposed to very heavy
rifle fire and machine gun fire, passed through into the N.W.
corner of the wood and established themselves in the wood,
being joined later by Lord Strathcona's Horse. Capt. Newcomen's
Squadron penetrated about half way up the S.W. face of the
wood, where they found heavy machine gun fire directed on
them from the enemy, between MORISEL and MORENIL. They turned
into the wood and established themselves. Major Timmis's
Squadron met with considerable opposition and wheeled to the
left, suffering very heavy casualties.

    Lord Strathcona's Horse (R.C.) were then ordered to send
one Squadron under Lieut Flowerdew to pass round the N.E.
corner of the wood at a gallop in support of Capt. Nordheimer,
while the remaining two Squadrons of the Regiment advanced to
the attack dismounted on the North Western face. Capt.
Nordheimer's Squadron got into the wood and engaged the enemy
in a hand to hand combat. Many of the enemy were killed all
refusing to surrender, but a large party, estimated about
300, retired from the wood S.E. of the point where Capt.
Nordheimer's Squadron had entered it. This party were charged
by Lieut Flowerdew (Lord Strathcona's Horse) and many of the
Germans were killed with the sword as they ran to meet the
Cavalry with the Bayonet, shewing no signs of surrender. Lieut
Flowerdew having passed through them, wheeled about to charge
again. He then gallope into the wood at the centre of the
Eastern face, established himself and was joined by the
Dismounted party of his Regiment. Fierce hand to hand fighting
ensued in all the N.W. part of the wood, resulting ultimately
in the complete capture of this portion of the wood and the
killing of all the German Garrison. The resistance of the
enemy was most stubborn; one badly wounded German, shot throug

both legs and the stomach, refused to allow the stretcher bearers move him, saying he would rather die uncaptured. Meantime, Capt. Newcomen's Squadron were held up half way down the Western face of the wood, and the enemy still held out in some strength in the S. point of the wood. Two Squadrons of Fort Garry Horse were sent to reinforce Capt. Newcomen, and a third Squadron of the same Regiment was sent across the river to enfilade the enemy from the high ground above MORISEL.

On the Northern face, 2 Squadrons of Lord Strathcona's Horse (R.C.) advanced dismounted Commanded by Lieut Col. McDonal, Many casualties were sustained in thsi advance and no doubt the whole party would have been destroyed had it not been for the simultaneous attacks on the enemy's rear, of which he was aware from the continous rifle and machine gun fire. Lieut Col. McDonald's party entered the wood and overcame any enemy resistance by 11 a.m. the attack having started at 9:30 a.m. the whole wood except the extreme Southern point was in possession of the Canadian Cavalry Brigade. The losses were severe, most Regiments having lost from half to one third of their Officers and a similar proportion of their men, and it would have been impossible to have held the wood but for the prompt arrival of General Bell-Smythe's Brigade who reinforced out weak points and bore the brunt of the fierce fighting later in the day in the wood. In spite of repeated counter-attacks by the enemy the wood was held by the Cavalry until 2:30 a.m. the following day, March 31st, when General Seeley handed over the defence of the captured wood, of which he had been placedd in charge to the Infantry of the 8th Division. On relief the Brigade retired and bivouacked in BOIS DE SENCAT, the Brigade H.Q. being established at CASTEL.

Throughout March 31st the Brigade stood to near BOIS DE SENCAT ready to assist the defence in case of counter attack but were not called upon.

B.   At 9:30 p.m. March 31st orders were received from the
2nd Cavalry Division, to which the Canadian Cavalry Brigade
were still attached, that the Division would counter-attack
at dawn the following day. The G.O.C. and Brigade Major
rode to GENTELLIES and attended a Conference lasting from
2 a.m. to 4 a.m. on April 1st, planning the attack. The attack
was to be made on RIFLE WOOD, one mile S. of HANGARD, which
had been occupied by the Germans. The command of the attacking
forces composed of the whole of the Dismounted men of the
2nd Cavalry Division, was given to the G.O.C. Canadian Cavalry
Brigade. The orders were drawn up and issued at 4 a.m. and
Commanding Officers of all Units were ordered to meet General
Seeley at DOMMARTIN at 7 a.m. The 4th Cavalry Brigade were
ordered to lead the attack on the road running due S. from
the Ridge at the N.E. corner of the wood to HANGARD. The 5th
Cavalry Brigade to seize the N.E. edge of the wood, and the
Canadian Cavalry Brigade to pass through the 5th Cavalry
Brigade and clear and occupy the wood. During this operation
the Canadian Cavalry Brigade was commanded by Lieut Col .
Peterson, D.S.O.

The operations were covered by all available Artillery
firing on laid down barrages, and also by concentrated
machine gun fire from the 3 Machine Gun Squadrons. The
Canadian Machine Gun Squadron was allotted the task of firing
on the N.E. face of the wood up to the last minute and then
gradually switching through the wood. These guns carried out
this difficult operation most effectively.

The attack started at 9 a.m. and was completely successful
although the losses were heavy. The whole of the wood was in
our possession by 11 a.m. There was much fierce fighting, but
the enemy showed more willingness to surrender than on the
30th March. Over 100 prisoners were taken and 13 machine guns.
Of these 13 machine guns 11 were used by the Hotchkiss Gunners
of the Canadian Cavalry Brigade against the enemy throughout
the day.

The positions round the wood were consolidated with the assistance of the 2nd Cavalry Division Field Squadron, commanded by Major Swinburn, who was killed while directing these operations. The enemy organised a strong counter attack of a whole Brigade, marching from VILLERS AUX ERABLES; they were observed concentrating by our air-men. Meantime the road and wood were very heavily shelled and the Oxfordshire Hussars and the 3rd Hussars on the left, and the 5th Cavalry Brigade and Canadian Cavalry Brigade suffered somewhat severely. Reinforcements were asked for. The Inniskilling Dragoons were sent forward to the wood and the Royal Scots Greys prolonged the flank from the wood in the direction of THENNES. The German counter attack, when launched, was completely repulsed and their losses were very severe, many hundreds of dead being left lying on the East and South of the wood.

The Canadian Brigade was relieved at 6 p.m. and marched to the BOIS DE SENCAT.

1.

CANADIAN CAVALRY BRIGADE.

NARRATIVE OF OPERATIONS for period 8th, 9th, 10th October 1918

8th October, 1918.

In accordance with Cavalry Corps orders, the Brigade being reserve Brigade to the 3rd Cavalry Division, assembled in the valley just S.W. of JONCOURT, the whole Division being in that neighbourhood supporting the 1st Cavalry Brigade Division, whose instructions were to pass through the Infantry on the line PREMONT-SERAIN being reached.

The Infantry obtained its objectives and the Brigade moved forward to the valley 3000 yards N.E. of BEAUREVOIR, with Brigade Headquarters at BRONX FARM (C.7.a.)

The R.C.Ds were detailed as Divisional left flank guard with orders to keep in touch with the advance of the 1st Division.

The 1st Division being unable to pass through the Infantry orders were received at 4:45 p.m. to return to bivouac in vicinity of BELLINCOURT-MAURGY, the march being made after dark.

The R.C.Ds suffered a number of casualties from shell fire and machine gun fire from hostile aircraft.

At 11:40 p.m. orders were received that the attack would continue in the morning with the 3rd Cavalry Division in the lead.

9th October.

The G.O.C. and Brigade Major attended a Conference at Divisional Headquarters at 4:00 a.m. and it was decided that the 7th Cavalry Brigade would lead with the 6th Cavalry Bde as right flank guard, one Regiment Canadian Cavalry Brigade as left flank guard, remainder of Canadian Brigade in Divisional Reserve.

In accordance with orders received the Brigade concentrated in the valley N. of BRONX FARM (C.1.c.) at 6 a.m. Brigade Headquarters being established with Divisional Headquarters at the Farm.

Information being received from returning wounded that the Infantry had pushed on as far as MARETZ without coming in touch with the enemy a motor cyclist was sent forward to ascertain the situation and he reported that he found the Infantry at the Eastern edge of MARETZ.

The Brigade was then moved forward about 2000 Yards along the valley to U.26.cent. and Brigade Headquarters moved the same distance along the MARETZ Road. The Divisional Commander came forward to that point.

Further information being received that the enemy had retired beyond MARETZ, and the 7th Cavalry Brigade not yet having arrived, the Divisional Commander, in conference with the Corps Commander, who had come up, decided to move forward on a two Brigade frontage, the Canadian Brigade to the N. of the LE CATEAU Road and the 6th Brigade to the S. the 7th Brigade coming into Divisional reserve, objectives as already laid down for Cavalry Corps, i.e. the high ground S.W. and N.W. of LE CATEAU to NEUVILLY, with a flank NEUVILLY-RAMBOURLIEUX FARM- TROISVILLES.

Brigade was disposed for this operation as follows:-
<u>Advance Guard</u>   F.G.H. 4 Machine Guns. "A" Battery R.C.H.A.
<u>Left Flank Guard</u> L.S.H. 4 Machine Guns.

Remainder of Brigade in support, moving parallel with and N. of MARETZ - LE CATEAU Road.

The left Regiment was instructed to move inside the line, CLARY-BERTRY-TROISVILLES, with reconnaissance to the line MONTIGNY-INCHY-NEUVILLY.

The Brigade moved forward at 9:30 a.m. and found the Infantry on the line, eastern edge of MARETZ-WOOD 1500 yards S.W. of L'EPINETTE-BOIS de PINCH, where they were held up by machine gun fire from the line BOIS GATTIGNY-VIARY.

The advance Regiment at this time had one Squadron at L'EPINETTE, the balance of the Regiment 1000 yards behind/with battery in action.

At 9:55 a.m. the L.S.H. reported that they were making

for high ground between BOIS de GATTIGNY and CLARY.

The Brigade Headquarters in the meantime had made three moves forward along the MARETZ Road with advance report centre on the MARETZ-CLARY Road 500 yards S. of l'EPINETTE.

At 11:10 a.m. F.G.H. reported that they had captured the western portion of the BOIS de GATTIGNY and BOIS-du-PONT-AUX-VILLES, but that the enemy were still holding that portion of the BOIS de GATTIGNY, bordering on the main road.

It later turned out that the F.G.H. had mistaken the Northern portion of BOIS GATTIGNY for BOIS-du-MONT-AUX-VILLES, and that the latter was still held by the enemy.

In this operation, which was supported by South African Infantry 200 prisoners, a 5.9 howitzer, a tank rifle, a trench mortar, and about 40 machine guns were captured by the F.G.H. and a large number of the enemy were killed with the sword.

At 11:10 the L.S.H. reported that 30 prisoners had been driven into the hands of the Infantry, that their advanced Squadron was on the high ground N.E. of CLARY (C.18Cenet) and that the enemy had retired to the northern edge of BOIS-du-MONT-AUX-VILLES (P.13.a. and b.) where their line was strongly held.

At 11:55 the F.G.H. reported that they had reached the small wood 1500 yards S. of BERTRY (P.20.d.9.0) and that they were held up by heavy machine gun fire from the direction of HONNECHY, and that their patrols reported that BERTRY was now clear except for a few machine guns.

At 12:25 p.m. the L.S.H. reported one Squadron in BOIS-du-MONT-AUX-VILLES, and that they were endeavouring to outflank the factory and farm on the BERTRY-CLARY Road about 1000 yards East of CLARY, (C.18.b.) They also reported that CLARY was clear and that our Infantry was entering the village.

At 12:30 p.m. the F.G.H. reported being held up in Railway cutting in valley S. of BETRY (P.21.a.) by machine gun fire coming from the South of the MARETZ-LE CATEAU Road.

At 11:15 Brigade report centre moved to farm S. of the road 500 yards from N.E. of MARETZ.

The Divisional General came forward to this point to ascertain the situation and held a conference of the Brigadiers of the 6th and Canadian Brigades, the 6th Brigade at this time having reached the valley 1000 yards N.E. of BUSIGNY-MARETZ Road. While the conference was in progress the farm was heavily shelled and there were a number of casualties to both men and horses.

It was decided that the 6th Brigade would encircle HONNECHY and seize the high ground between that place and REUMONT, and that the Canadian Brigade would encircle MAUROIS from the N. connecting with the 6th Brigade between that point and REUMONT.

The Brigade Report Centre was moved to the X Roads on the MARETZ-BERTRY Road on S. edge of BOIS GATTIGNY, and the Brigadier went forward to the F.G.H. H.Q. in P.20.d. On arrival there he found that the F.G.H. had taken MAUROIS and were holding along the line of the MAUROIS-BERTRY Road, and that the South African Scottish were taking over the village, but that HONNECHY was still held by the enemy. During this operation one Squadron (Major Mills) working to the North of MAUROIS charged the enemy about P.16.cent. capturing 40 prisoners and 3 machine guns.

In the meantime the L.S.H. had captured the factory and farm on the BERTRY-CLARY Road with 42 prisoners and 5 machine guns and had entered the W. edge of BERTRY.

Brigade Report Centre was now moved forward to small wood 1500 yards S. of BERTRY, and the main body, which was in the valley N.W. of MARETZ was ordered forward to BOIS de GATTIGNY.

1:00 p.m. A message was received from the 6th Cavalry Brigade that they had been obliged to retire behind the line of the BUSIGNY-MARETZ Road owing to heavy shelling, the Royal Dragoons being left forward immediately behind the Infantry who were holding the line of the Railway.

Two Squadrons of the F.G.H. being held up on the MAUROIS

-BERTRY Road owing to heavy machine gun and shell fire from the direction of REUMONT and the high ground South of the road between HONNECHY and that point, the Brigadier ordered one Squadron of the R.C.Ds (Major NEWCOMEN) to swing round the left of the F.G.H. getting in touch with the L.S.H. at BERTRY, to seize the high ground N. of REUMONT.

The reserve Squadron of the F.G.H. to describe a smaller circle and enter REUMONT from the N.W. The other two Squadrons which were dismounted, to conform to the movement and endeavour to enter the village along the road. Orders were sent to the L.S.H. to clear BERTRY and push on to TROISVILLES, in order to cover the flank of this movement.

For this operation all the Artillery (R.C.H.A. Brigade, with one Battery of 4.5 Howitzers attached) was grouped in the valley 1000 yards W. of MAUROIS, and they, with all the available machine guns, were put into action covering the manoeuvre. This operation which was entirely successful, resulted in the capture of the line East exit of REUMONT-l'SOTIERRE at the N.E. exit of TROISVILLES.

Major Newcomen's Squadron reached its objective in time to cut off the enemy retiring from REUMONT, capturing an Officer, 29 O.R's, and 3 machine guns and killing a number of the enemy with the sword.

Major Strachan F.G.H. succeeded in entering REUMONT dismounted Major Mill's was wounded, the L.S.D. captured le FAYT at 3:55 p.m. and moved through and to the E. of TROISVILLES.

During this operation Brigade Report Centre moved to a point on the MAUROIS-BERTRY Road, 800 yards from MAUROIS X-roads and the main body was ordered forward to the valley of the l'ERCLIUM.

About 3:30 p.m. word was received from the Division that Fourth Army reported enemy guns and transport retiring down the INCHY-LE CATEAU Road to LE CATEAU, and 4.5 Howitzers were put on the HALTE, S.E. of INCHY, and that the main X-roads W. of LE CATEAU, orders being sent to the L.S.H. at 3:45 p.m.

to get across the INCHY - LE CATEAU road as soon as possible. This road was also engaged with 13 pdr. shrapnel, the R.C.H.A. Batteries being moved to a forward position for this purpose.

As the F.G.H. were now somewhat scattered they were ordered to assemble in support in the valley at Northedge of REUMONT, the R.C.Ds being ordered to pass through and seize that portion of the final objective between the MONTAY and RAMBOURLIEUX FARM, the L.S.H. to hold from HAMBOURLIEUX FARM to TROISVILLES.

Brigade Report Centre moved forward to the high ground on the road 500 yards N.E. of REUMONT, and the Brigadier went forward to Colonel Straubenzee, who by this time had reached the valley S. of small wood 800 yards N. of REUMONT. Colonel Straubenzee having received his instructions was on his way to rejoin his Regiment when he was killed by a shell which also seriously wounded his Adjutant. Major Newcomen was at once placed in Command and instructed to get in touch with the L.S.H. at TROISVILLES, and reach his objective by an encircling movement via RAMBOURLIEUX FARM. By this time it was quite dark and this most successful operation was carried out with great judgment under most difficult conditions. Major Newcomen established his Headquarters 800 yards S.E. of RAMBOURLIEUX FARM, the Headquarters of the L.S.H. being at the farm at the time. and the line was held from the high ground near the road 500 yards S.W. of Montay-X road N.W. of RAMBOURLIEUX FARM - along the road to LA SOLTIERES, with cossack posts and standing patrols well forward. R.C.Ds patrols entered MONTAY and patrolised the Southern MONTAY-NEUVILLY Road to the L.S.H. on their left. L.S.H. patrols entered NEUVILLY and reported that place strongly held N. of the River. Some of our Infantry entered NEUVILLY during the night but later retired. L.S.H. patrols also entered INCHY. Brigade Intelligence Officer visited NEUVILLY and INCHY and confirmed these reports.

Owing to the right flank being open from the N. edge of REUMONT (where the 6th Brigade had been relieved by the 6th Corps Cyclists) to LE CATEAU, the F.G.H. (less one Squadron which was kept as Brigade Reserve) was ordered forward to support the right of the R.C.Ds.

Regimental Headquarters were established near the X roads 1000 yards S.W. of PONT DES @ VAUX, one Squadron forward at the latter point with patrols into LE CATEAU and in touch with the R.C.Ds. near MONTAY, and with the 3rd Dragoon Guards on the main road 2000 yards N.E. of REUMONT, the 7th Brigade having come up in support and having detailed one Squadron of the 3rd Dragoon Guards to connect from the left of the 6th Brigade to the right of the F.G.H.

These posts were maintained until daylight although some of them were heavily shelled. The F.G.H. and L.S.H. suffered a number of casualties to men and horses.

At daylight (10th) the Brigade withdrew to the valley E. of TROISVILLES, having been relieved by the 7th Cavalry Brigade and Infantry.

Three armoured Cars were detailed to operate with the Brigade but did not report. They were seen working through the road in the BOIS de GATTIGNY, but were apparently unable to get further owing to the craters in the road.

Attached map shows movements of troops and situations at various periods.

10th October.

At 2:15 p.m. the Brigade (less R.C.H.A.) moved back to MONTIGNY, the R.C.H.A. being divisionalised to assist the Infantry attack. During this operation Major McPherson, "B" Battery R.C.H.A. and one other rank was killed, and one other rank wounded.

The Brigade during the above operations advanced about 8 miles after passing through the Infantry and cleared for that distance a strip of country nearly 5 kilometres wide. The rapidity of the advance prevented the enemy from destroying a number of villages, although he had made preparations to do so, and released a large number of civilian who received our men with open arms and furnished a great deal of valuable information of the movements and intentions of the enemy.

A large number of the enemy were killed, over 400 prisoners (including a number of Officers), several guns of different calibres, some trench mortars, tank rifles, two motor cars, and nearly 100 machine guns were captured.

The casualties in the Brigade, during this operation were comparatively light, consisting of the following:-

Lieut. Col.	Straubenzee	R.C.D.	Killed
Lieut.	Welsh	L.S.H.	Killed
Lieut.	Cruickshank	R.C.H.A.	Wounded
Lieut.	James	R.C.D.	Wounded
Lieut.	Richmond	L.S.H.	Wounded
Lieut.	Finnigan	L.S.H.	Wounded
Major	Middlemast	F.G.H.	Wounded (at duty)
Major	Mills	F.G.H.	Wounded
Lieut	Black	F.G.H.	Wounded
Lieut	Dunwoody	F.G.H.	Wounded
Lieut	Griffin	M.G.S.	Wounded
Lieut	Tucker	M.G.S.	Wounded

Other Ranks.

	Killed.	Wounded.	Missing.
R.C.H.A.	-	4	-
R.C.D.	1	5	15
L.S.H.	9	42	-
F.G.H.	14	34	2
M.G.S.	2	13	2
Brigade HQ & Signals.	2	3	-

Horse Casualties.

Killed 109.   Wounded 40,   Missing 22.

(sgd) R.W.Paterson
Brigadier General, Commanding
Canadian Cavalry Brigade.

Confidential.

Vol 44

War Diary
of
Canadian Troops
3rd Cavalry Division.

Intelligence Summaries
May 1918

Confidential.

(6339) Wt. W160/M3016 1,500,000 10/17 McA & W Ltd (E 1898) Forms W3091.　　Army Form W.3091.

Cover for Documents.

Nature of Enclosures.

Notes, or Letters written.

LIST of APPENDICES.

Appendix No.

1.	... ...	3rd Cav. Div. G.A.70 dated 3.5.18.
2.	... ...	do. do. Order No.28 d/3.5.18.
3.	... ...	do. do. G.A.82 dated 4.5.18.
4.	... ...	do. do. Order No.29 d/4.5.18.
5.	... ...	do. do. G.S.104/1 d/4.5.18.
6.	... ...	Fourth Army 42/22(G) dated 5.5.18.
7.	... ...	3rd Cav. Div. Order No.30 d/5.5.18.
8.	... ...	do. do. G.A.87 dated 5.5.18.
9.	... ...	do. do. G.A.88 " 5.5.18.
10.	... ...	do. do. G.S.104/2" 5.5.18.
11.	... ...	do. do. G.M.3. " 6.5.18.
12.	... ...	do. do. G.A.93 " 6.5.18.
13.	... ...	do. do. G.110/1 " 8.5.18.
14.	... ...	do. do. G.S.110/3" 9.5.18.
15.	... ...	do. do. G.S.110/4" 9.5.18.
16.	... ...	do. do. G.A.127 " 9.5.18.
17.	... ...	do. do. G.S.111/1" 10.5.18.
18.	... ...	do. do. Order No.31 d/15.5.18.
19.	... ...	do. do. G.A.59 dated 21.5.18.
20.	... ...	do. do. Order No.32 d/22.5.18.
21.	... ...	do. do. do. 33 d/29.5.18.

"A" Form
MESSAGES AND SIGNALS.

Army Form C.2121 (in pads of 100).

Appendx 1

TO	3rd Fd. Sqdn.	C.R.H.A.	O.C.A.S.C.
	3rd Sig. Sqdn.	A.D.M.S.	A.P.M.
	D.A.C.	A.D.V.S.	

Sender's Number.	Day of Month.	In reply to Number.	AAA
G.A.70.	3rd.		

Division will be prepared to move 8.30 a.m. tomorrow 4th inst. to new area AAA Detailed orders follow AAA Addsd. all concerned.

Will O.C. A.S.C. please inform Reserve Park which will probably not move till 9.0 or 9.30 a.m. or perhaps later.

From: 3rd Cav. Div.
Time: 8.45 p.m.

(Sd) J.A. MUIRHEAD, Lt. Col.

Appendix 2

S E C R E T.   Copy No. _____

3rd CAVALRY DIVISION ORDER No. 28.

3rd May, 1918.

Reference Maps 1/100,000.
Sheets HAZEBROUCK 5.A. & LENS 11.
----

1. 3rd Cavalry Division will move tomorrow May 4th to an area east of HESDIN in accordance with March Table overleaf.

2. Intervals of 300 yards will be observed between Squadrons and similar units and 100 yards between every 20 vehicles.
    French Artillery will be moving across line of march

3. A. and B. Echelons will accompany Brigades.

4. Divisional H.Q. will close at PERNES and open at WAIL at 12-noon on 4th instant.

            R.O.Cecil Major
            for Lieut-Colonel,
        General Staff, 3rd Cavalry Division.

Issued at 11-55.,pm.

Copies to :- 1. 6th Cavalry Brigade.
      2. 7th Cavalry Brigade.
      3. Canadian Cavalry Brigade.
      4. 4th Brigade R.H.A.
      5. 3rd Signal Sqdn R.E.
      6. 3rd Field Sqdn R.E.
      7. 3rd Cav. Res. Park.
      8. D.A.C. (RCHA Bde Amm Col attd)
      9. A.A.& Q.M.G.
      9. A.D.M.S.
     10. A.D.V.S.
     11. A.P.M.
     12. O.C.A.S.C.
     13. Camp Commandant.
     14. Cavalry Corps.)
     15. XIII Corps.   ) for information.
     16. First Army.   )
     17. Third Army.   )

March Table issued with 3rd Cavalry Division Order No. 28.

Serial No.	Unit.	Date.	From.	To	Starting Point	Time	Route	Remarks
1.	7th Cav. Bde.	May 4th	PERNES - BOYAVAL area.	LINZEUX, BLANGERVAL, AUBROMETZ, HARAVESNES, HAUT MAISNIL, Pt. FILLIEVRES.	Selected by Brigade.	8.30 a.m.	TANGRY - RAVRANS - BEAUVOIS	
2.	Canadian Cav. Bde.	"	PREDEFIN - VERCHIN area.	NEULETTE, NOVELLE les HUMIERES, FRESNOY, VIEIL HESDIN, ST. GEORGES, VACQUERIETTE.	do.	8.30 a.m.	BLANGY sur TERNOISE.	
3.	6th Cav. Bde.	"	NEDONCHELLES Area.	MONCHEL, CONCHY sur CANCHE, BOUBERS sur CANCHE, VACQUERIE LE BOUCQ, ROUGEFAY.	do.	8.30 a.m.	PERNES - VALHUON - ST.POL - FLERS.	
4.	3rd Field Sqdn.R.E.	"	SAINS les PERNES	OEUF.	SAINS les PERNES.	10 a.m.	As for Serial 1.	
5.	3rd Cav.Res.Park.	"	do.	GUINECOURT.	do.	10.30 a.m.	do.	To follow D.A.C.
6.	D.A.C. (R.C.H.A.Bde.Ammn. Col. attached)	"	PRESSY les PERNES.	OEUF.	PRESSY les PERNES.	10 a.m.	do.	To follow 3rd Fd. Sqdn.
7.	Div. H.Q. Details.) H.Q.4th Bde.R.H.A.) " A.S.C.) " A.H.T.)	"	PERNES	MAIL.	PERNES.	9.30 a.m.	Any.	

"A" Form
MESSAGES AND SIGNALS.

Army Form C. 2121 (in pads of 100).

This message is on a/c of Appendix 3

| TO | All concerned. | | |

Sender's Number.	Day of Month.	In reply to Number.	AAA
* G.A.82.	4th		

Units will be prepared to march at 7 A.M. tomorrow AAA New area not yet settled AAA Details will be issued later AAA The above does not apply to 6th Brigade which will march in the afternoon.

From: 3rd Cav. Div.
Place:
Time: 6.55 p.m.

(sd) R.S.P. WOOD, Capt.

Appendix H

Copy No. 19

S E C R E T.

3rd Cavalry Division Order No. 20.

4th May, 1918.

Reference Maps 1/100,000,
Sheets LENS & ABBEVILLE.
----

1. 3rd Cavalry Division will move tomorrow 5th May to a staging area east and south-east of AUXI-LE-CHATEAU in accordance with March Table overleaf.

2. Intervals of 300 yards will be observed between Squadrons and similar units and 100 yards between every 30 vehicles.

3. A. and B. Echelons will accompany Brigades.

4. Divisional Headquarters will close at WAIL at 12-noon and re-open at YVRENCH at the same hour on the 6th instant.

5. ACKNOWLEDGE.

J.W. Muirhead

Lieut-Colonel,
General Staff, 3rd Cavalry Division.

Issued at .... p.m.

Copies to :- 1. 6th Cav. Bde.
2. 7th Cav. Bde.
3. Candn. Cav. Bde.
4. 4th Brigade R.H.A.
5. 3rd Field Sqdn R.E.
6. 3rd Signal Sqdn R.E.
7. 3rd Cav. Res. Park.
8. D.A.C.(R.C.H.A.Bde.Amm.Col.attd.).
9. "Q"
10. A.D.M.S.
11. A.D.V.S.
12. A.P.M.
13. O.C.A.S.C.
14. Camp Commdt.
15. Cavalry Corps.
16. Third Army.
17. Fourth Army.

March Table issued with 3rd Cavalry Division Order No. 29.

Serial No.	Unit.	Date.	From.	To.	Route.	Remarks.
1.	7th Cav. Bde.	5th	HAUT MAISNIL - BLANGERVAL.	BEAUVOIR RIVIERE, BEAUCOURT, ST. ACHEUL, LE MEILLARD, HEUZECOURT, MONTIGNY-LES-JONGLEURS, MAIZICOURT.	BUIRE-AU-BOIS - NOEUX - NAVANS.	To be S. of the FREVENT-HESDIN Road by 7.45 a.m.
2.	Canadian Cav. Bde.	5th	VIEIL HESDIN area.	LONGVILLERS, MESNIL, DOMQUEUR, DOMQUEUR, LE PLOUY.	VACQUERIETTE - GUQEUX - AUXI LE CHATEAU and any route to the N. of it.	To be S. of the FREVENT-HESDIN Road and by 8 a.m.
3.	6th Cav. Bde.	"	BOUBERS area.	VACQUERIE-LE-BOUCQ, BOFFLES, FORTEL, NOEUX, VILLIERS, L'HOPITAL, NAVANS, BEAUVAIS, NAVANS.	Any.	FREVENT-HESDIN Road to be left clear for French between 8 A.M. and 2 P.M.
4.	3rd Fd. Squadron R.E.	"	OEUF.	YVRENCHEUX.	HAUT MESNIL - LE PONCHEL.	To be S. of FREVENT-HESDIN Road by 7.50 a.m. To follow units of 7th Cav. Bde.
5.	3 Div Ammn. Col.	"	OEUF.	do.	do.	To be S. of FREVENT-HESDIN Road by 8 a.m. To follow 3rd Fd. Sqdn.
6.	3rd Cav. Res. Park. (Light Section)	"	GUINECOURT.	VAULX.	HAUT MAISNIL	March at 1.30 p.m. To join heavy Section 3rd Cav. Res. Pk. at VAULX.
7.	Div. H.Q. Details. H.Q. 4th Bde. R.H.A. " S.C. " A.H.T.	"	WAIL.	YVRENCH.	Any.	March at 9 a.m.

Appendix 5

S E C R E T.
x 6th Cavalry Brigade.   x D.A.C.
x 7th Cavalry Brigade.   x 3rd Cav.Reserve Park.
x Canadian Cav. Brigade.   A.D.M.S.
  C.R.H.A.   A.D.V.S.
x 3rd Field Squadron R.E.   O.C. A.S.C.
x 3rd Signal Squadron.   Camp Commandant.

G.S.104/1
4.5.18.

W A R N I N G   O R D E R.

The Division will move on the 6th May to a bivouac area about BLAUCOURT SUR L'HALLUE (2 miles S.W. of CONTAY) and be in Fourth Army reserve in III Corps area.

Detailed orders will be issued later when area has been notified.

Units should be ready to move at 7 A.M. on 6th May, as the march is a long one and an early start will probably be necessary.

J. Muirhead.
Lieut.-Colonel,
G.S., 3rd Cavalry Division.

4th May, 1918.

x S.D.2.

Issued at 10-25 p.m.

SECRET.   Fourth Army No. 42/22(G).

x x x
III Corps.
Cavalry Corps.
----

1. III Corps will take over the northern portion of the Australian Corps front between the following boundaries, as shewn on attached map:-

   Southern Boundary.
   The E. and W. grid line running from the front line through D.23.a.0.0. to A.23.b.8.0.(junction with French Area).

   On the North.
   Present boundary between Fourth and Third Armies.

2. Command will pass from Australian Corps to III Corps on 6th instant at an hour to be arranged between Corps and notified to A.H.Q.

3. On completion of relief H.Qs. will open as follows:-

   III CORPS   -   VILLERS BOCAGE.
   AUST.CORPS -   BERTANGLES.

4. The counter-battery boundary between III and Australian Corps will be the E. and W. grid line through D.23.a.0.0.(Sheet 62D).

5. III Corps will take over and administer the troops now under the orders of the Australian Corps, as detailed in Appendix "A".

6. The following will be the distribution of the Tank Corps in Fourth Army:-

   A.H.Q.
   5th Tank Brigade H.Q.   MOLLIENS AU BOIS.

   In Army Reserve.
   1st Tank Bn.(Mark IV).   (½ Bn. BOIS MADAME (I.9.a.)
                                            (½ Bn. FRANVILLERS.

   Affiliated to III Corps.
   No.2 Tank Bn.(Mark V)   )
       (less 1 Co.)   )   BAIZIEUX WOOD (C.11.a. & c.)
   1 Co. 3rd Tank Bn.   )
       (Whippets).   )   WARLOY.

   Also 1 Co. Whippets under Third Army at WARLOY can be called through Fourth Army.

   Affiliated to Australian Corps.
   No.8 Tank Bn. (Mark V).   Wood in N.34.c.
   1 Co. No.2 Tank Bn.(Mk.V).   MERICOURT - BONNAY area.

7. 3rd Cavalry Division will arrive in the III Corps area on 6th May and be accommodated in the HALLUE Valley. It will be held in Army Reserve.

8. Acknowledge by wire.

H.Q., Fourth Army,   (Sd) A.A.MONTGOMERY, Major General,
4th May, 1918.   General Staff, Fourth Army.

(issued with Fourth Army No.42/22 (G)
dated 4.5.18.)

APPENDIX "A".

18th Division (less Artillery).
47th Division (less Artillery).

Artillery Units.

    18th Divisional Artillery.
    96th Army Brigade R.F.A.
    169th   do.
    282nd   do.
    5th Army Brigade R.H.A.

    76th Brigade R.G.A. (Mixed).
    85th   do.   (Mobile).
    89th   do.   (How. 8").
    98th   do.   (How. 9.2").
    449th Siege Battery (6" Gun Mk.XIX).

R.E. Units.

    288th A.T.Co. R.E.
    221st   do.
    1st Siege Co. R.A.R.E.
    180th Tunnelling Co.R.E.

    253rd Tunnelling Co. R.E. will join III Corps from Fourth Army on 6th May.

R.A.F.Units.

    35th Squadron R.A.F.

Anti-Aircraft Unit.

    "Q" A.A.Battery.

Administrative Units. (including Labour Units).

    As notified by Fourth Army "Q".

Appendix 7

SECRET.   Copy No........

3rd Cavalry Division Order No.30.

Reference Maps 1/100,000:-
  ABBEVILLE, 14.
  LENS, 11.   5th May, 1918.
  AMIENS, 17.
----

1. 3rd Cavalry Division will continue the march tomorrow, 6th May, to its final area - CONTAY and BEHENCOURT - in accordance with March Table overleaf.

2. Following intervals will be observed:-

   Between Squadrons and similar units   ...   300 yards.

   "   Batteries R.H.A. and columns of
       20 vehicles   ...   .   100 yards.

3. A and B Echelons will accompany units.

4. 3rd Cavalry Reserve Park, H.Q. Aux. H.T. Company and heavy sections Cavalry Field Ambulances will move in accordance with instructions issued separately.

5. Divisional Headquarters will close at YVRENCH and open at CONTAY at 2 p.m. 6th inst.

6. Acknowledge.

                                    (sgd) Neil Major
                                    for Lieut.Colonel,
                                    G.S., 3rd Cavalry Division.

Issued at 8.40 p.m.

Copies to:-
1 to 6th Cav. Bde.   10 to A.D.V.S.
2   " 7th   "   11 " A.P.M.
3   " Canadian Cav. Bde.   12 " O.C. A.S.C.
4   " 4th Bde. R.H.A.   13 " Camp Commandant.
5   " 3rd Fd.Sqdn. R.E.   14 " Cav. Corps.   )
6   " 3rd Signal Sqdn.   15 " Third Army.   ) for
7   " D.A.C.   16 " Fourth Army.   ) information.
8   " A.D.M.S.   17 " III Corps

March Table issued with 3rd Cavalry Division Order No.30.

Serial No.	Unit.	From.	Starting Point's	Time =	= Route =	Remarks.
1.	Canadian Cav. Bde.	BERNEMCOURT	DOMQUEUR Ch'ch [?] end	8 p.m.	ETINEHEM-LES-DOMART-VIGNACOURT-VILLERS BOCAGE-MOLLIENS AU BOIS.	To be clear of VIGNACOURT at 11 p.m.
2.	7th Cav. Bde.	do.	As selected by Bde.	do.	BERNEVILLE-C.NEMS-Fme. du ROSEL-HERISSART.	Troops less Echelon B to be E. of CONTAY Church by 4 p.m.
3.	6th Cav. Bde.	do.	do.	do.	FROHEN le GRAND-DOULLENS-M.SON AR.-BEAUQUESNE-TOUTENCOURT.	To enter CONTAY from the West & not to cross the HERISSART-CONTAY road before 4 p.m.
4.	3rd Field Sqdn R.E.	BERNCOURT	As for Serial No.1	9 a.m.	As for Serial No.1	To follow Canadian Cav. Bde.
5.	Div. Ammn. Col. A.S.C.	do.	do.	9.20 a.m.	do.	To follow Serial No.6.
6.	Div. Head Details H.Q. 4th Bde. R.C.H.A. A.S.C.	do.	do.	9.10 a.m.	do.	To follow 3rd Fd. Sqdn.

"A" Form
MESSAGES AND SIGNALS.
Army Form C. 2121 (in pads of 100).

TO: All concerned.

Sender's Number.	Day of Month.	In reply to Number.	AAA
G.A.87	May 5th		

Ref. 3rd Cav. Div. Order No.30, para. 4 AAA 3rd Cav. Res. Park, of H.Q. of A.H.T.Company and Heavy Sections of C.F.A. will move from present areas on 6th inst. to BEALCOURT 4 miles S.E. of AUXI-LE-CHATEAU AAA No movement before 12 Noon AAA Heavy Sections C.F.A. to move under orders of affiliated Brigades AAA Addsd. all Brigades, 3rd Cav. Res. Park, O.C. A.S.C. reptd. A.D.M.S. A.A. & Q.M.G. and 3rd Signal Squadron.

From: 3rd Cav. Division.
Time: 8.25 p.m.

(Sd) R.E. CECIL, Major, G.S.

"A" Form
MESSAGES AND SIGNALS.

Army Form C. 2121 (in pads of 100).

Appendix 9

TO:
3rd Cav. Res. Park through Cav. Cav. Corps.
A.A. & Q.M.G.
O.C. A.S.C.

Sender's Number: G.A.88
Day of Month: May 5th
AAA

Warning Order AAA Reference G.A.87 of 5th inst. AAA Light Section 3rd Cav. Reserve Park will continue march to join Division on 7th inst AAA Orders follow AAA Addsd. 3rd Cav. Res. Park reptd. A.A. & Q.M.G. and O.C. A.S.C.

From: 3rd Cav. Div.
Time: 10.45 p.m.

(Sd) R.E. CECIL, Major,

S E C R E T.

Appendix 10

3rd Cavalry Division.

    The 4th Brigade R.H.A. will remain with the 3rd Cavalry Division in Army Reserve.

    In the event of a Battle, the Brigade may be allotted to either the III or Australian Corps and be employed under their orders.

    The O.C. 4th Brigade R.H.A. should be instructed to report personally to the G.Os. C.R.A. of the III and Australian Corps, in order to receive instructions as to the role that may be allotted to his Brigade and to make the necessary reconnaissances.

5th May, 1918.
HT.

                                                  (Sd) ------------
                                                         Major General,
                          General Staff, Fourth Army.

Copy to III Corps.
       Aust. Corps.
       G.O.C. R.A.

-2-

4th Brigade R.H.A.

    For information.

                                       (Sd) J.A.MUIRHEAD,
                                              Lieut.Colonel,
5.5.18.   G.S., 3rd Cavalry Division.

"A" Form
MESSAGES AND SIGNALS.

Army Form C. 2121
(in pads of 100).
No. of Message..............

Appendix 11

TO: 3rd Cav. Res. Park.

Sender's Number.	Day of Month.	In reply to Number.	AAA
G.M.3.	6th		

In continuation of my G.M.2. AAA
Third Army have given BEALCOURT to you for
tonight so you can move Heavy and Light
Sections there in accordance with original
order AAA Am trying to get a place in the
Fourth Army area to move your Heavy Section
to tomorrow and will let you know later AAA
Light Section Reserve Park will move tomorrow
7th May to BEHENCOURT (3 miles S. of CONTAY)
AAA Send representative of Light Section
to be at BEHENCOURT Church at 12 noon tomorrow
7th to meet Divisional Staff Officer who will
allot billets AAA H.Q. Aux. H.T.Coy. will
remain with your Heavy and Light Sections
today and move with them wherever they go AAA
Will you inform O.C. Aux. H.T. AAA If you do
not receive orders to move your Heavy Section

/2

"A" Form
MESSAGES AND SIGNALS.

Army Form C. 2121
(in pads of 100).

Sender's Number.	Day of Month.	In reply to Number.	AAA
G.M.3.	6th		

from BEALCOURT tomorrow you will know that
3rd Army have given permission for it to
remain there for present but it will be more
convenient to have it further South and hence
endeavour is being made to get a place for it.

From 3rd Cav. Div.
Time 12.50 P.M.

(Sd) J.A.MUIRHEAD,

G.S.

"A" Form
MESSAGES AND SIGNALS.

Army Form C. 2121 (in pads of 100).

Appendix 12

TO	3rd Cav. Res. Pk.	A.D.M.S.
	A.A. & Q.M.G.	Heavy Section C.F.A.
	O.C.A.S.C.	

Sender's Number.	Day of Month.	In reply to Number.	AAA
G.A.93	May 6th		

Heavy Section Res. Park, Heavy Section Cav. Field Ambce. and H.Q. Aux. H.T. will move tomorrow 7th to SURCAMPS (2 miles W. of DOMART) AAA Light Section Reserve Park will move tomorrow 7th to BEHENCOURT (3 miles S. of CONTAY) AAA No restrictions as regards roads or times AAA Intervals of 400 yards between every 12 transport vehicles AAA Billets at SURCAMPS to be arranged mutually AAA Addsd. 3rd Cav.Res.Park and Heavy Section C.F.A. (by Special D.R.) repeated all concerned.

From 3rd Cav. Div.
Place
Time 6.25 P.M.

(Sd) J.A. MUIRHEAD, Lt.Col

Appendix 13

III Corps No.G.O.9441/2.

x x x x
3rd Cavalry Division. (for information).

In amplification of para. 9 (b) of III Corps Provisional Defence (No.G.O.9441), the Corps Commander wishes Divisions as under to consider the action they would take to meet any of the following eventualities, and to carry out reconnaissances, and prepare schemes for this purpose.

<u>18th Division.</u> (1) The recapture of (a) Spur D.12.7.13.
                    "   "   " (b) LAVIEVILLE.
                    "   "   " (c) Spur D.16.22.

              (2) Forming a defensive flank
                 (a) Facing S.E. if right flank about BUIRE is turned.
                 (b) Facing N.E. if enemy occupies the Spur in V.30.W.25 or MILLENCOURT.
                 (c) If HENENCOURT and MILLENCOURT are taken.

<u>47th Division.</u> (1) The recapture of (a) Spur V.30.a.b. - W.25.a.b.
                    "   "   " (b) MILLENCOURT.
                    "   "   " (c) HENENCOURT.

              (2) Forming a defensive flank
                 (a) Facing N.E. covering HENENCOURT and MILLENCOURT.
                 (b) Facing S.E. in the event of LAVIEVILLE being taken by the enemy.

<u>58th Division.</u> (1) Reconnaissance with a view to driving the enemy back if he has penetrated on to the ridge running N. and S. through LAVIEVILLE and in particular detailed plans for the recapture of
                 (a) HENENCOURT.
                 (b) LAVIEVILLE.
              (2) Ejecting the enemy, if he has obtained a footing in the BAZIEUX defences or the WARLOY Sector.
              (3) The occupation of the FRANVILLERS-CONTAY defences.

H.Q., III Corps.   (Sd) C.G.FULLER,
7th May, 1918.   B.G.G.S., III Corps.

-2-

6th Cavalry Brigade.
7th Cavalry Brigade.   <u>G.110/1.</u>
Canadian Cavalry Brigade.   8.5.18.

        For information.

8th May, 1918.   (Sd) J.A.MUIRHEAD, Lieut.Col.,
                                General Staff, 3rd Cavalry Division.

Appendix 14

SECRET.

6th Cavalry Brigade.	3rd Field Squadron R.E.	
7th Cavalry Brigade.	3rd Signal Squadron.	G.S./10/3
Canadian Cavalry Brigade.	"Q".	9.5.18.
4th Brigade R.H.A.	A.D.M.S.	

In the event of the 3rd Cavalry Division being placed at the disposal of the III Corps, their general employment may be visualised as follows:-

1. If circumstances and time permit, it is the intention to pass the Reserve Infantry Brigades of the Division in Corps Reserve through the Cavalry, and to keep the Cavalry behind, mounted, for an emergency.

2. If a break through or a critical situation arises, which will not allow time for the Infantry Reserves to get up, then one or more Cavalry Brigades will be called upon to restore the situation at that point, and to hold the gap or ground regained until the Infantry arrive, when the cavalry will rejoin their horses.

3. The gap or critical situation indicated in para. 2 may occur on any part of the Corps front, and the Cavalry Brigades should be prepared accordingly to move to any portion of the front. If, however, the Reserve Infantry Brigades have passed through and reached the BAIZIEUX system, then the Cavalry are more likely to be required to protect one flank or the other from a turning movement by the enemy.

4. In consequence:-

   (a) The two Cavalry Brigades not employed in digging during the night on the HENENCOURT defences will "stand to" saddled up from 5 A.M. until 8 A.M. "B" Echelons will be packed but will not "stand to".

   (b) The Cavalry Brigade engaged in digging on the HENENCOURT defences will remain at two hour's notice unless orders to the contrary are issued.

5. It is essential that, whether the Cavalry have been called upon to move or not, routes should be kept clear for the Reserve Infantry Brigades (173rd and 174th Brigades of 58th Division) to move forward. These brigades will move to initial positions of assembly as under:-

   173rd Infantry Brigade group. - C.20.

   Route. - Cross roads D.11.d. - MONTIGNY - BEHENCOURT.

   174th Infantry Brigade group. - C.5.

   Route. - BEAUCOURT - CONTAY and tracks leading eastward from latter village.

6. In either of the cases mentioned in paras. 2 or 3 above, all Whippet Tanks available are to be placed at the disposal of the 3rd Cavalry Division to assist in the operation. H.Q. of O.C. Whippets is at V.19.c.5.6.

7. Reconnaissances will continue to be carried out of the main defensive positions and of the approaches and crossings.

Lieut. Colonel,
G.S., 3rd Cavalry Division.

9.5.18.

Copy to:- III Corps.   58th Divn.
         18th Divn.   O.C. Whippets.
         47th Divn.

"A" Form
MESSAGES AND SIGNALS

Appendix 15

Army Form C. 2121
(in pads of 100)

TO	6th Cav. Bde.
	7th Cav. Bde.
	Canadian Cav. Bde.

Sender's Number.	Day of Month.	In reply to Number.	
G.S.110/4	9th		AAA

Ref. this Office G.S.110/3 para. 4 (a) the two Cavalry Brigades will be saddled up by 5 A.M. and will offsaddle and be at one hour's notice from 5.30 A.M. until 8 A.M. when they will come on to two hours notice.

From: 3rd Cav. Div.
Place:
Time: 9 a.m.

(Z)
(Sd) J.A. MUIRHEAD, Lt.Col.

Wt. W492/M1647 100,000 pads. 4/17. W. & Co., Ltd. (E. 1187.)

"A" Form
MESSAGES AND SIGNALS.

Army Form C. 2121
(in pads of 100).

Appendix 16

TO:
- 6th Cav. Bde.
- 7th Cav. Bde.
- Canadian Cav. Bde.

Sender's Number.	Day of Month.	In reply to Number.	AAA
G.A.127.	9th		

Until further orders commencing on 10th May each Brigade will provide one Officer's patrol of one officer and ten other ranks to report at Divisional H.Q. to General Staff at 6 a.m. daily AAA This patrol will be returned during the morning if the tactical situation does not require their employment.

From Place: 3rd Cav. Div.
Time: 2.30 P.M.

(Sd) J.A. MUIRHEAD, Lt. Col.

S E C R E T.

Appendix II

6th Cavalry Brigade.
7th Cavalry Brigade.
Canadian Cavalry Brigade.
C.R.H.A.

G.S.111/1
10.5.18.

1. The following are the general principles of defence of the III Corps front:-

(a) The Front Line is the main line of Resistance, and will be held. Should the enemy penetrate into any portion of it, Divisional and Local Commanders will at once organize counter-attacks to regain the lost ground. Should the counter-attack fail, every effort will be made to prevent the enemy extending his gains, and to clear up the situation in order to facilitate a deliberate counter-attack with adequate artillery preparation and assisted by tanks.

(b) The BAIZIEUX System South of a line drawn East and West through U.29.central and the WARLOY System from the Northern Corps boundary to its junction with the BAIZIEUX System in D.7.a. will be held by a permanent garrison of 1 Brigade provided by the Division in Corps Reserve and the 34th M.G. Battalion, under orders of G.O.C. Reserve Division. 1/1st Northumberland Hussars will be responsible for the defence of the BAIZIEUX System North of a line drawn East and West through U.29.central.
  O.C. 1/1st Northumberland Hussars will be prepared to garrison this line at short notice with dismounted portion of the regiment.
  The BAIZIEUX and WARLOY Systems will be used as a rallying place for stragglers, etc. and as a jumping-off place for counter-attack to regain any ground which may have been temporarily lost.
  The permanent garrison of these systems will be not employed for counter-attack.

(c) The Reserve Line of the Front Zone (LAVIEVILLE - MILLIE- WALLABY - POSSUM Trenches) will be held by a permanent garrison of 2 Battalions, one of which may be a Pioneer Battalion, and at least 2 Sections of Machine Guns, in each Divisional Sector. These garrisons will not be used for counter-attack until and after they have been replaced by a similar number of troops from Divisional or Corps Reserve.

2. With reference to this Office G.S.110/3 of 9.5.18, para.5, two Battalions of the 173rd Infantry Brigade have now moved to C.20.b., and two Battalions of the 174th Infantry Brigade have already moved to the vicinity of C.5. The remaining Battalions of the above Brigades are shortly to move forward to the above positions from the MIRVAUX - MOLLIENS AU BOIS area where they are at present located.
  The restriction placed on the Canadian Cavalry Brigade not to use the route via BEHENCOURT (see G.A.119 to Canadian Cav.Bde.)is now removed.
  The 58th Division (173rd, 174th and 175th Brigades) is the Division in Corps Reserve; the 175th Infantry Brigade is at present the Brigade referred to in para. 1 (b) above.

3. Demolition of Bridges.

(a) C.E., III Corps will be responsible for the preparation and carrying out of all demolitions of bridges, and blowing up of road craters in the Corps area.

(b) C.E. III Corps will maintain parties to carry out the demolitions in the immediate vicinity of the place where the demolition is required, and he will notify the Divisions concerned of the exact location of these parties, and to whom the order for demolition is to be sent.

(c) Bridges will only be destroyed under the following conditions:-
  (i) On the written orders of an Officer not below the rank of Brigadier General.
  (ii) In the event of our Infantry having retired across the bridge, the latter coming under direct rifle or machine gun fire.

(d) The fact of any bridge having been destroyed will be immediately reported to III Corps.

........Tanks.

-2-

4. Tanks.

The following are the III Corps instructions for the employment of Tanks.

(a) The following Tanks are allotted to III Corps, and are located as under:-

2 Coys. No.2 Tank Battn.(18 - Mk.V Tanks)(H.Q. at FRECHENCOURT).
"A" Coy.-BAIZIEUX ORCHARD (C.5.d.)affiliated to 47th Division.
"B" Coy.-S.end of BAIZIEUX Wood(C.11.d.) affiliated to 18th Division.
1 Coy.9th (Light) Tank Battn. (12 Whippets) - WARLOY.

The Hd.Qrs. of the O.C. 5th Brigade Tanks, is at VAUX-EN-AMIENOIS.

(b) The Mk.V Tanks are to be utilised to counter-attack, accompanied and supported by Infantry, in order to restore the situation along the Corps front.
They are not to be frittered away in twos or threes for regaining small portions of trench, which may have been lost, etc. but as far as possible are to be used in a body with an organised Infantry attack.

(c) Mk.V Tanks will also be used to counter-attack any German Tanks. In the event of information being received of a hostile attack with tanks, Divisions will order their affiliated Mk.V Tanks forward to attack them, informing Corps Hd.Qrs. of their action. The Company Commanders, No.2 Tank Battn., will attack any hostile Tanks that may be reported to them, without waiting for orders from Corps or Divisional Hd.Qrs. and will report this action to Divisional H.Q.

(d) The Whippet Coy. will operate independently of the Infantry. Should a break have occurred in the line, they will be sent out to ascertain the situation, to break up any hostile massing, and thus to gain time for the organized counter-attack.

(e) Tanks are under Corps orders and with the exceptions detailed in para. 4 (c) are not to be utilised without sanction from Corps Headquarters.

NOTE: Para. (d) to be read in conjunction with this Office G.S.110/3, para.6.

5. Withdrawals.

III Corps instructions regarding withdrawal are as under:-

It is to be impressed on all ranks that the present front system is where it is intended to give battle to the enemy, and that it is the Corps Commander's intention to put in , if necessary, the whole force at his disposal to hold on to our present line.

It is, however, necessary to be prepared for unexpected eventualities, and three Zones of Defence are consequently in preparation.

Should our present line be driven back by weight of numbers, Divisions will occupy the successive lines of defence in the areas comprised in their Divisional boundaries, contesting every inch of the ground.

(Sd) J.A.MUIRHEAD, Lieut.Col.,
10th May, 1918.   G.S., 3rd Cavalry Division.

Appendix 18

ORDERS.

3rd Cavalry Division Order No. 31.

Reference Maps 1/100,000 AMIENS, LENS
& ABBEVILLE Sheets.   15th May, 1918.

1.   The 3rd Cavalry Division (less Canadian Cavalry Brigade, R.C.H.A.Brigade and Ammunition Column, and 1 Field Troop R.E.) will march on 17th May to an area about ST.OUEN and BELLOY-SUR-SOMME, in accordance with March Table overleaf.

2.   Canadian Cavalry Brigade with R.C.H.A.Brigade and Ammunition Column, and 1 Field Troop R.E. attached, will remain in their present area West of BEHENCOURT.

3.   Details now at SURCAMPS will move to BETHENCOURT ST.OUEN, marching at 4 P.M. on 17th May under the orders of O.C. Heavy Section 3rd Cavalry Reserve Park.

4.   Intervals will be maintained on the march in accordance with Fourth Army Standing Orders, Part I, Para. 358 (D.R.O.2892 dated 14.5.18).

5.   The 3rd Cavalry Division will continue to be administered by the III Corps.

6.   Divisional Headquarters will close at CONTAY and open at YZEUX at 10 a.m. on 17th May.

7.   Units of 3rd Cavalry Division to acknowledge.

                                                    Lieut.Colonel,
Issued at ......6.30......P.M.   G.S., 3rd Cavalry Division.

Copies to:-
1 to 6th Cav. Bde.
2 " 7th Cav. Bde.
3 " Canadian Cav.Bde.
4 " 3rd Fd.Sqdn.R.E.
5 "   3rd Signal Sqdn.
6 " Div. Amm.Col.
7 " Light Sec. 3rd Cav.Reserve Pk.
8 " "Q".
9 " C.R.H.A.
10 " A.D.M.S.
11 " A.D.V.S.
12 " O.C. A.S.C.
13 " Camp Commandant.
14 " Fourth Army.
15 " III Corps.
16 " Cav. Corps.
17 " 18th Division.
18 " 47th Division.
19 " 58th Division.
20 " A.P.M.

March Table Issued with 3rd Cavalry Division Order No. 31.

Serial No.	Unit.	From	To	Starting Point.	Time.	Route.	Remarks.
1.	6th Cav. Bde.	CONTAY.	BELLOY-SUR-SOMME.	Cross Roads ½ mile S.W. of BEAUCOURT Church.	—	Cross roads 1 mile N. of ST. GRATIEN Church - RAINNEVILLE - COISY - BERTANGLES - VAUX-EN-AMIENOIS - ST.SAUVEUR.	To be clear of Starting Point by 7.15 A.M. To be W. of AMIENS-DOULLENS Road by 9.45 a.m.
2.	7th Cav. Bde.	"	ST.OUEN.	As selected by Brigade.	—	RUBEMPRE - VILLERS BOCAGE - VIGNACOURT.	Not to enter VILLERS BOCAGE before 11.15 a.m.
3.	3rd Fd.Sqdn. (less 1 Troop).	BEHENCOURT	BETHENCOURT ST.OUEN.	As for Serial No.1.	7.20 a.m.	As for Serial No.1 as far as BERTANGLES, thence via VIGNACOURT.	To be W. of BERTANGLES, AMIENS-DOULLENS road by 10 a.m.
4.	Div.Amm. Column (less R.G.H.A. Bde. Amm.Col.)	"	"	"	7.30 a.m.	"	To be W. of AMIENS-DOULLENS Road by 10.15 a.m.
5.	Light Section, 3rd Cav.Reserve Park.	"	YZEUX.	"	7.50 a.m.	"	To be W. of AMIENS-DOULLENS Road by 10.30 a.m.
6.	Divisional H.Q. H.Q. 4th Bde.R.H.A. H.Q. A.S.C.	CONTAY.					will be notified separately.

"A" Form
MESSAGES AND SIGNALS.

Army Form C. 2121 (in pads of 100).

Appendix 19

TO: 7th Cavalry Brigade.
Canadian Cavalry Brigade.

Sender's Number.	Day of Month.	In reply to Number.	AAA
G.A.59	21st		

7th Cavalry Brigade will relieve the Canadian Cavalry Brigade in the forward area on the 24th May AAA orders for move will follow in due course AAA K Battery, one Field Troop R.E. and one section D.A.C. will move with 7th Cav. Bde. and Canadian Cav. Bde. will return complete with the Field Troop and Canadian R.H.A. Brigade and Ammn. Column now attached to it.

From: 3rd Cav. Div.
Place:
Time: 11.50 p.m.

(Sd) J.A. MUIRHEAD, Lt.Col.

Appendix 20

SECRET.   Copy No........

<u>3rd Cavalry Division Order No. 32.</u>

Reference Maps 1/100,000, LENS & AMIENS Sheets.   May 22nd, 1918.

1. 7th Cavalry Brigade with 1 Field Troop and 1 Section Divisional Ammunition Column attached will relieve Canadian Cavalry Brigade Group in forward area on May 24th in accordance with March Table overleaf.

2. 7th Cavalry Brigade Group on arrival in BEHENCOURT Area will come under orders of III Corps and will report arrival direct to III Corps.

3. Canadian Cavalry Brigade will hand over all details regarding work, etc., and Fourth Army S.O.S. Signals, to 7th Cavalry Brigade on relief.

4. Movement whenever possible will be by existing tracks at side of road.

5. Canadian Section of Divisional Ammunition Column and Field Troop R.E. will rejoin Divisional Ammunition Column and 3rd Field Squadron respectively on arrival at BETHENCOURT ST.OUEN.

6. Acknowledge.

                                                   Lieut.Colonel,
Issued at 12.15 P.M.   G.S., 3rd Cavalry Division.

Copies to:-
1. to 7th Cavalry Brigade.   11. to A.D.M.S.
2. " Canadian Cav. Bde.   12. " A.D.V.S.
3. " C.R.H.A.   13. " A.P.M.
4. " 3rd Field Squadron.   14. " O.C. A.S.C.
5. " D. A. C.   15. " Camp Commdt.
6. " 6th Cav. Brigade.   16. " Fourth Army.
7. " 3rd Signal Squadron.   17. " III Corps "G".
8. " 3rd Cav.Res. Park.   18. " III Corps "Q".
9. " Aux. H.T. Coy.   19. " Cavalry Corps.
10. " "Q"   20. " Australian Corps.

March Table issued with 3rd Cavalry Division Order No.32.

Unit.	Date.	From.	To.	Route.	Remarks.
7th Cav. Brigade Group.	May 24th	ST.OUEN area C.	BEHENCOURT area.	VIGNACOURT - FLESSELLES - MOLLIENS AU BOIS - X roads ½ mile N. of ST. GRATIEN.	Xroads ¾m N of To reach/ST. GRATIEN at 11.30 a.m. Field Troop and Section D.A.C. will move under orders of 7th Cav. Brigade.
Canadian Cav. Bde. Group.	May 24th	BEHENCOURT area	ST.OUEN area C. and BEHENCOURT ST.OUEN for Canadian Sect. D.A.C. & Field Troop R.E.	x roads ½ mile N. of ST.GRATIEN - X roads ½ m. W. of ST. GRATIEN -RAINNEVILLE - COISY - BERTANGLES - X roads ½ mile S.S.W. of VAUX-EN-AMIENOIS - X roads 2 miles W. of VIGNACOURT.	Head to pass X roads ½ mile N. of ST. GRATIEN at 10 A.M. and column to clear that point by 11.30 A.M.

Appendix 21

SECRET.   Copy No.........

3rd Cavalry Division Order No.33.

Reference Maps 1/100,000 LENS & AMIENS Sheets.   May 29th, 1918.

1.   6th Cavalry Brigade with 1 Field Troop and 1 Section Divisional Ammunition Column attached will relieve 7th Cavalry Brigade Group in forward area on May 31st in accordance with March Table overleaf.

2.   6th Cavalry Brigade Group on arrival in BEHENCOURT area will come under the orders of III Corps and will report arrival direct to III Corps.

3.   7th Cavalry Brigade will hand over all details regarding work, etc. and Fourth Army S.O.S. Signals to 6th Cavalry Brigade on relief.

4.   Movement whenever possible will be by existing tracks at side of road.

5.   The Section, Divisional Ammunition Column and Field Troop R.E. now attached to 7th Cavalry Brigade will rejoin Divisional Ammunition Column and 3rd Field Squadron respectively on arrival at BETHENCOURT ST. OUEN.

6.   Advance parties of 6th and 7th Cavalry Brigades will proceed on May 30th to take over tents, etc. and bivouac area.
       Advance party of 7th Cavalry Brigade will ascertain location of training area now used by 6th Cavalry Brigade.

7.   Acknowledge.

                                              J.G. Howhs Major
                                              for   Lieut.Colonel,
Issued at .....3.....P.M.   G.S., 3rd Cavalry Division.

Copies to:-
   1. 6th Cav. Bde.   13. A.P.M.
   2. 7th Cav. Bde.   14. O.C. A.S.C.
   3. Candn. Cav. Bde.   15. Camp Commdt.
   4. 3rd Fd. Sqdn.   16. Fourth Army.
   5. 3rd Signal Sqdn.   17. III Corps G.
   6. Div. Ammn. Column.   18. III Corps Q.
   7. 3rd Cav. Res. Park.   19. Cavalry Corps.
   8. Aux. H.T. Company.   20. Australian Corps.
   9. "Q"   21. 18th Division.
  10. C.R.H.A.   22. 47th Division.
  11. A.D.M.S.   23. 58th Division.
  12. A.D.V.S.

March Table issued with 3rd Cavalry Division Order No.33.

Serial No.	Unit.	Date.	From	To	Route.	Remarks.
1.	6th Cavalry Brigade Group.	May 31st.	BELLOY SUR SOMME (ST.OUEN area A.)	BEHENCOURT area.	ST.SAUVEUR - BERTANGLES - VILLERS BOCAGE - MOLLIENS AU BOIS - X roads ½ mile North of ST. GRATIEN.	Head of column to reach X roads ½ mile North of ST.GRATIEN at 11.30 a.m. Field Troop and Section D.A.C. will move under orders of 6th Cav. Bde.
2.	7th Cavalry Brigade Group.	"	BEHENCOURT area.	BELLOY SUR SOMME (ST.OUEN area A.)	X roads ½ mile North of ST. GRATIEN - RAINNEVILLE - COISY - BERTANGLES - ST.SAUVEUR.	Head of column to pass X roads ½ mile North of ST.GRATIEN at 10 a.m. and column to clear that point at 11.15 a.m. Field Troop & Section D.A.C. may leave column at X roads 1 mile S.S.W. of VAUX-EN-AMIENOIS, thence via ST.VAST and X roads 2 miles West of VIGNACOURT to BETHENCOURT ST.OUEN.

www.ingramcontent.com/pod-product-compliance
Lightning Source LLC
Chambersburg PA
CBHW081542160426
43191CB00011B/1819